Charles H. Thompson on Desegregation, Democracy, and Education

Charles H. Thompson on Desegregation, Democracy, and Education

1953–1963

Louis Ray

FAIRLEIGH DICKINSON UNIVERSITY PRESS
Vancouver • Madison • Teaneck • Wroxton

Published by Fairleigh Dickinson University Press
Copublished by The Rowman & Littlefield Publishing Group, Inc.
4501 Forbes Boulevard, Suite 200, Lanham, Maryland 20706
www.rowman.com

6 Tinworth Street, London SE11 5AL, United Kingdom

Fairleigh Dickinson University Press gratefully acknowledges the support received for scholarly publishing from the Friends of FDU Press.

British Library Cataloguing in Publication Information Available

Library of Congress Control Number: 2020934308

ISBN 978-1-61147-991-1 (cloth : alk. paper)
ISBN 978-1-6114-7993-5 (pabk : alk. paper)
ISBN 978-1-61147-992-8 (electronic)

∞™ The paper used in this publication meets the minimum requirements of American National Standard for Information Sciences Permanence of Paper for Printed Library Materials, ANSI/NISO Z39.48-1992.

This book is dedicated to my mother, Hattie Hobbs
to my wife, Muriel A. S. Grimmett,
and to the memory of my mentors, Carroll Lee Liverpool Miller and
Henry J. Perkinson

Contents

Acknowledgments

The support of family, colleagues, and friends has made *Charles H. Thompson on Desegregation, Democracy, and Education: 1953–1963* a reality. Professors Robert Carter and David Julian Hodges provided the spark, mentoring, and model for this journey. The example of scholarship and friendship demonstrated by the late Henry J. Perkinson, David M. Reimers, and James R. Bliss, who were the outstanding scholars who guided me through the dissertation process at New York University, continues to inspire me. It has been my good fortune to receive counsel and support from Derrick P. Alridge, James D. Anderson, John H. Bracey Jr., Bettye Collier-Thomas, Lenwood G. Davis, V. P. Franklin, Karen Graves, Evelyn Brooks Higginbotham, Walter Johnson, David Levering Lewis, Monroe H. Little, Catherine A. Lugg, Christopher M. Span, Adah Ward Randolph, Gayle T. Tate, Maurice Isora Mitchell Williams, and Francille Rusan Wilson.

Much of what I learned about Charles H. Thompson came from reading his articles, correspondence, and editorials. A fuller understanding of Thompson's project, however, came after interviewing several scholars who knew and worked with him, such as the late John Hope Franklin, the late Carroll Lee Liverpool Miller, and the late Rachel T. Weddington. I am also indebted to Theresa Rector and Michael R. Winston for sharing their perspectives that were crucial to my understanding of Thompson's approach to education and race relations. Clifford L. Muse, Jr., and Joellen ElBashir transformed my visits to the Howard University Archives and Howard University's Moorland-Spingarn Research Center, respectively, into intellectually stimulating experiences: I thank them for their patience and confidence in me.

Words cannot convey my appreciation for the vision, editorial skills, commitment, and scholarship of Lilith M. Haynes, who sharpened this study's focus and argument much as she did that of the first volume. I am also thankful for the support that *The Journal of Negro Education*'s Lenda P. Hill, Cynthia J. Joseph, and Ivory A. Toldson have continually demonstrated in my research. The Fairleigh Dickinson University (FDU) Press, its editorial board, editor emeritus Harry Keyishian, editor James Gifford, and Louise Stahl have been steadfast in their commitment to my scholarship. I thank them and the team at The Rowman & Littlefield Publishing Group, Inc., led by associate editor Zachary Nycum, for all of their efforts in publishing this book.

The collections and librarians of Fairleigh Dickinson University, the New York Public Library, and the Schomburg Center for Research in Black Culture also were invaluable to this project. Many of its chapters first appeared as papers that I presented at scholarly societies such as the Association for the Study of African American Life and History, the American Educational Studies Association, the History of Education Society, and the International Standing Conference for the History of Education. I am appreciative of the support of the colleagues at these professional associations who made these presentations possible, and travel grants from Fairleigh Dickinson University that helped finance my attendance at these meetings.

The students with whom it was my privilege to work as a TRIO director for the Research Foundation–The City University of New York and as a faculty member at FDU's Peter Sammartino School of Education have contributed much to my personal and intellectual development. I have enjoyed working with them as well as my colleagues at FDU, especially Vicki Cohen, Carol F. Karpinski, Marlene Rosenbaum, and Miriam J. Singer. My church family at the Abyssinian Baptist Church led by the Reverend Dr. Calvin O. Butts III, has strengthened my connection to African American education, history, culture, and religion. My mother, Hattie Hobbs, modeled a belief in the liberating possibilities of education; Mom, I admire your example of courage, tenacity, and love. I received a first-class education because of your efforts at home and the efforts at school of the excellent teachers of the Niagara Wheatfield School District. Last, but not least, I thank my wife, Muriel A. S. Grimmett for her boundless wisdom, insight, "can-do" spirit, and love. I am solely responsible for any mistakes or omissions in this book.

Preface

Robert Russa Moton and Jennie Dee, his second wife, had retired to Holly Knoll, their spacious Georgian Revival home in Gloucester, Virginia, in the same year that Thompson published the 1935 issue of the Yearbook, *The Courts and the Negro Separate School*. For decades, Moton had been a towering figure in US race relations, having succeeded Booker T. Washington as the principal of Tuskegee Institute in Alabama and as the leader of what remained of Washington's vaunted, and much feared, political machine known as the "Tuskegee Machine." Holly Knoll was located at 6496 Allmondsville Road, overlooking the York River, and according to journalist Denise Watson, "Moton turned the construction of the house over to Hampton and Tuskegee students . . . [and decided to name the estate] Holly Knoll for the proliferation of greenery on its grounds." In time, the home featured a swimming pool and tennis courts, twelve bedrooms, and nearly as many bathrooms, and its "second-story balcony [ran] the length of the house, and the upstairs rooms all [emptied] onto it"—all of which encouraged conversations. Indeed, the Motons' "famous [and coveted] invitation 'Come to Cappahosic' brought many friends and colleagues from near and far to discuss and resolve issues affecting the African-American community, especially in the field of education."[1]

Responding to their invitation, some of Afro-America's leading educators, artists, intellectuals, entertainers, and activists came to Holly Knoll to swim, play tennis, read, converse, and plan the direction of the unfolding civil rights movement. Noted for their hospitality, the Motons made people, regardless of their political leanings, feel welcome; indeed, they had designed their space to facilitate the intellectual "border crossings" that are so essential for building alliances. These deliberations, in turn, contributed to the launch of the United Negro College Fund, the direct attack on the constitutionality of segregation, and proposals for strengthening African American higher education during the early years of desegregation. On the grounds of Holly Knoll, the guests planned voter registration drives in the South and the student-led sit-in movement. Most significant, as Watson also noted "under the secrecy of night," white progressives often crossed the York River to join the guests at Holly Knoll in forging some of these developments.

After R. R. Moton's death in 1940, his vision continued as Frederick D. Patterson, Moton's son-in-law and successor as principal or president of Tuskegee Institute, converted Holly Knoll into the Moton Conference

Center and added dormitories to accommodate even more guests. Today, Holly Knoll has landmark status, but from 1935 to the early 1960s, it was a prime gathering place for the African American intelligentsia: on its grounds, they could freely discuss solutions to vexing educational and race relations problems. Such was its significance in Afro-America that for nearly three decades the presidents of the African American colleges or historically black colleges and universities made the pilgrimage to Cappahosic three times annually.[2]

The word "Cappahosic" appeared only once in the writings of Charles H. Thompson, the editor of *The Journal of Negro Education* and subject of this book: in his "Editorial Note: The Negro Private and Church-Related College," published in summer 1960.[3] However, an exchange of letters between Thompson and Horace Mann Bond, dean of the Atlanta University School of Education, suggested that this omission was deliberate on Thompson's part. In a letter dated October 30, 1959, Thompson wrote, "Dear Horace: It was nice seeing you at the Cappahosic conference a few weeks ago and doubly pleasant to have you as a guest during the period."[4] On November 18, 1959, Bond wrote in reply, "I am as usual overdue in acknowledging the great comfort, ease, and relaxation I enjoyed at your Cappahosic villa. Please accept my gratitude, and convey these sentiments to Mrs. Thompson."[5]

In other words, when Bond attended "the Cappahosic conference" on the African American private and church-related colleges, he had been a guest of the Thompsons who had earlier purchased a summer home near Cappahosic so that Thompson could participate in the discussions occurring at Holly Knoll. A maxim that Thompson scrupulously observed throughout his career was that to have your voice and ideas count, you must be present when and where the negotiations on pressing issues occurred. The Thompsons had saved money from their salaries as teachers and bought this summer home near Gloucester, Virginia, to ensure that Thompson and other leading African American educators were present at the meetings convened at Cappahosic. Following the example set by the Motons, the Thompsons hosted other African American scholars so that they, too, could participate in these deliberations. They also saved enough for Thompson to travel to meetings at the National Association for the Advancement of Colored People Legal Defense and Educational Fund, Inc., the launch of United Negro College Fund at Tuskegee Institute in 1943, and the halls of Congress, to name a few. The Thompsons had established this practice early in their marriage, and they paid all or part of the expenses for Thompson to bring the inequitable state of African American education to the attention of the attendees of the World Federation of Education Associations held at Oxford University, Oxford, England, in mid-August 1935.[6] By supporting these initiatives, they demonstrated their belief in African American self-determination and their hope that world opinion would have a decisive role in extending African

Americans' civil rights domestically and human rights for all "subject and underprivileged peoples" internationally.

This book, *Charles H. Thompson on Desegregation, Democracy, and Education: 1953–1963* completes an intellectual biography of Charles Henry Thompson's editorship of *The Journal of Negro Education* that my first book, *Charles H. Thompson: Policy Entrepreneur of the Civil Rights Movement, 1932–1954* (2012), began. Both of these works assess Thompson's contributions to US education through the lens of his work as a leading policy entrepreneur, or, to use John Kingdon's definition, his work "as an advocate distinguished by . . . singular willingness to invest their resources—time, energy, reputation, and sometimes money" to realize their vision of a desired public policy.[7] As noted earlier, the goals of achieving equal citizenship rights for African Americans and international respect for human rights and the rule of law inspired Thompson to focus his energies first on ending segregation as public policy in the United States. From 1926 to 1963, he tirelessly championed equal educational and economic opportunity for African Americans and other targets of discrimination. *Charles H. Thompson: Policy Entrepreneur of the Civil Rights Movement, 1932–1954*, captured Thompson's model of advocacy and scholarly activism as African American teachers assumed a substantial role in the struggle for legal equality during the Great Depression, World War II, and the early years of the postwar period. The reward for their efforts, after nearly a quarter-century of struggle, was *Brown v. Board of Education of Topeka* (1954), the landmark Supreme Court decision declaring racial segregation in public education in the United States illegal. This milestone was the conclusion of my previous book, and it serves as the introduction to this one: *Charles H. Thompson on Desegregation, Democracy, and Education: 1953–1963*.

This study examines the decade following *Brown II* (1955), a period characterized by tepid support for civil rights and educational equity by the federal government which it felt would allow the Southern states the time to make the administrative and other adjustments necessary for making the transition to a unitary public school system. As this study shows, Thompson's response to the resistance by Southern whites to nullify desegregation was not resignation; instead, he continually identified opportunities for advancing the desegregation and civil rights movements. As Thompson correctly anticipated, periods of reaction often followed on the heels of periods of progress in the United States, and these two volumes highlight the centrality of historical analysis to Thompson's project. Carefully chronicling the ebb and flow of the civil rights struggle from a leading African American educator's perspective, Thompson's editorials reflected his optimism that the proponents of equality would prevail if they selflessly devoted their resources, time, thinking, and energy to the civil rights struggle, and used the intelligent application of political pressure to win concessions from political and economic elites.

As a means of examining Thompson's primary method for periodically assessing progress and for identifying, selecting, and "timing" the issues that he felt were "ripe" for social action, the narrative in *Charles H. Thompson on Desegregation, Democracy, and Education: 1953–1963* features the Yearbook issues of the *Journal*. This study's treatment of the Yearbooks distinguishes the second volume by not only addressing this gap in the literature but also demonstrating Thompson's brilliance in defining African American education broadly and conceiving of the African American civil rights movement as one aspect of the international struggle for human rights. As Thompson explained in his editorial note to the 1943 issue of the Yearbook, *The American Negro in World War I and World War II*:

> The *Journal* has always conceived education to be a social process as broad as life itself, and assumes that the definition of our educational problems depends on an understanding of the social background and setting of those problems. Hence any problem of Negro life involving social adjustment is, according to our assumptions, a proper subject for the *Journal*. [Moreover,] one of the major weaknesses of the Negro's effort toward betterment of his status in America has been the fact that he has viewed his special disabilities in too narrow perspective, both temporally and geographically. It is too easy for the present generation to assume that all their woes began with them or reached their greatest intensity in their day. It is likewise too easy to fall into the error of attempting to evaluate one's progress from observation of the current scene without benefit of historical or geographical perspective.[8]

It is worth noting that Thompson's emphasis in these Yearbooks was not on publishing new research but on presenting critical analyses, interpretations, and syntheses of the relevant contemporaneous literature. He sought to tease practical solutions from existing knowledge and rather than "reinventing the wheel," he adopted the recurring ten-year reviews and assessments that Du Bois had initiated when publishing his Atlanta University studies. For Thompson, debates and critical assessments were methods for not only for gleaning insights from the literature that might have otherwise gone unnoticed; such discussions and assessments were also tools for forging a consensus regarding promising policy solutions that might energize the fight for civil rights and propel it forward.

NOTES

1. Denise Watson, "If the Civil Rights Movement had a home, it was here," February 20, 2011, *The Virginian-Pilot*, accessed July 14, 2018, https://pilotonline.com/guides/african-american-today/article_2f6a81f0-584c-54dc-b99e-5da0cda9dfa0.html; "Holly Knoll," Virginia Foundation for the Humanities, accessed July 14, 2018, http://www.aahistoricsitesva.org/items/show/208.

2. Gloucester Institute, "The Moton Center," accessed July 14, 2018, https://www.gloucesterinstitute.org/the-moton-campus.

3. Charles H. Thompson, "Editorial Note: The Negro Private and Church-Related College," *The Journal of Negro Education*, 29, no. 3 (Summer 1960): 211.

4. Charles H. Thompson, letter to Horace Mann Bond, October 30, 1959, School of Education Papers, Moorland-Spingarn Research Center, Howard University Archives, Howard University, Box 1894, *Journal of Negro Education*.

5. Horace Mann Bond, letter to Charles H. Thompson, November 18, 1959, School of Education Papers, Moorland-Spingarn Research Center, Howard University Archives, Howard University, Box 1894, *Journal of Negro Education*.

6. Sterling A. Brown, Arthur P. Davis, and Ulysses Lee, editors, *The Negro Caravan* (New York: The Citadel Press, 1941), 937.

7. John W. Kingdon, *Agendas, Alternatives, and Public Policies*, second edition (New York: Longman, 2003), 122–24.

8. Charles H. Thompson, "Editorial Note: The American Negro in World War I and World War II," *The Journal of Negro Education*, 12, no. 3 (July 1943): 266.

Introduction

Reversing Segregation as Public Policy

As Charles H. Thompson, editor of *The Journal of Negro Education* (hereafter the *Journal*), wrote the introductory sentences of his winter 1954 editorial in longhand, each word connected him to important aspects of the civil rights movement that had begun nearly twenty years earlier. More than two decades had passed since October 1931 when Thompson had founded the *Journal* at Howard University: a scholarly magazine that published quarterly issues in the winter, spring, and fall and was highlighted by the Yearbook issue published each summer. The *Journal* soon established itself as "one of the finest publications of its kind" in historian Richard Bardolph's estimation and according to journalist Richard Kluger, "Rarely has a scholarly publication served a more immediately useful practical purpose."[1] Kluger further noted that:

> Though he had no money except to pay the printing bills and the postage, [Thompson] launched the *Journal* as a means of fully documenting the conditions of Negro schools and exploring the implications of segregated education. Thompson's magazine now seized the torch that had been let fall when [Du Bois resigned as editor of] *The Crisis*. . . . The *Journal* was, to be sure, far less polemical than *The Crisis* had ever been, but it served a similar purpose: to inform, to arouse, [and] to inspire.[2]

Throughout his forty-year career, Thompson had unapologetically championed the use of hard data to make decisions and policies that would be for "the good of Negro education as a whole."[3] He reputedly advised his students to "get the facts, get the facts, and the rest would take care of itself," sure that gathering the facts was a necessary step to developing interpretations and conclusions that were consistent with that evidence. As Thompson developed the *Journal* into a scholarly journal that was attractive to African American scholars, the caliber of its scholarship also gained the respect of mainstream scholars and policymakers. So extensive were Thompson's social networks and so solid was his reputation as a scholar and educational insider that Thompson persuaded educators, including established leaders in their disciplines, and "educational experts across the country, white as well as Negro" to contribute regularly to the *Journal*.[4] Colleagues who knew Thompson described him as someone continually in search of new talent. He was particularly receptive to emerging scholars irrespective of race, gender, or nationality, and he frequently enlisted the support of others in identifying them. A review of the *Journal* during Thompson's years offers ample evidence of his success in cultivating emerging scholars many of whom went on to distinguished careers.

By early 1953, Thompson's *Journal* had survived the perils of the Great Depression, World War II, McCarthyism, and the crises of the postwar period. It also had survived recurring episodes of budget-cutting and belt-tightening on the Howard campus, and during those years it also cemented its reputation as "an invaluable chronicle of almost every development in black education of any consequence," according to Kluger.[5] Moreover, under Thompson's leadership, the *Journal* cultivated a coherent literature documenting the history of the pervasive educational discrimination experienced by African Americans in the segregated states. Its pages regularly featured critical commentaries and assessments of proposals, whether they were well-meaning or not, and whose very formulation often worsened African Americans' bleak prospects for gaining a fair share of the nation's educational resources. Thompson's editorials and articles also frequently served as lightning rods prodding African Americans and progressives to assert themselves through lobbying and practical politics to build support for more favorable educational and social policies.

In early December 1953, the twentieth anniversary of the publication of the 1935 issue of the Yearbook, *The Courts and the Negro Separate School,* was approaching. That issue of the Yearbook had gone to press one month after Charles Hamilton Houston had resigned as vice dean of the Howard University School of Law in June 1935 in order to serve as the special counsel to the National Association for the Advancement of Colored People (NAACP) Legal Defense Fund. Contrary to the depiction extended by its opponents, Howard University was not a sanctuary for radicalism; instead, its climate was portrayed as moderate and even conservative by eyewitnesses such as Dr. Rachel Weddington, an undergraduate at Howard during the 1930s and a former student of Thompson's who became a distinguished professor. Weddington pointed out that only a handful of faculty members engaged in civil rights protests, and those who did so were mainly a "group of senior, independent-minded professors [such as Houston and Thompson] . . . who felt secure enough to be activists."[6] She recalled that Houston and Thompson "stood out as leaders of the effort to increase the involvement of Howard students, faculty, and administrators in civil rights."[7] As self-respecting [citizens] of a democracy, Houston and Thompson believed that African Americans should not stop fighting until they gained the full rights of American citizens.[8]

When Charles Hamilton Houston assumed leadership of the NAACP Legal Defense and Educational Fund, Inc., in 1935, opinion in Afro-America was badly split over the potential for using the NAACP litigation campaign to expand educational opportunities and civil rights, generally, for African Americans. Educational discrimination in the Southern states had grown markedly since 1900, in conjunction with a precipitous decline in African Americans' civil rights: in such a climate, Thompson believed that a thorough examination of the strengths and limitations of litigation as a method for ending unlawful discrimination was necessary. Therefore, when designing *The Courts and the Negro Separate School*, he had assembled some of the foremost critics and proponents of litigation for a paper-based symposium to engage in a debate capable of deciding its potential for reducing racial discrimination in the segregated states. Accordingly, the ensuing 1935 Yearbook "was full of the "bright and provocative" pieces that Benjamin Brawley had advised Thompson to make the *Journal*'s trademark.[9]

The Courts and the Negro Separate School had succeeded admirably in challenging the objections leveled against litigation by radicals such as Du Bois and Ralph J. Bunche and conservatives such as W. B. T. Williams of Tuskegee. Making the case for litigation were philosopher Alain Locke, Gladys Peterson (an African American public school teacher), and attorneys Maceo W. Hubbard and Raymond Pace Alexander, who believed that it was possible to use litigation based on the due process and equal protection clauses of the Fourteenth Amendment to reduce racial discrimination in the South. In his chapter, "Court Action the Only Reasonable Alternative to Remedy Immediate Abuses of the Negro Separate School," Thompson pointedly suggested that African Americans had to use every legitimate means of redress at their disposal. Because only a handful of African Americans in the Southern states could vote, and removing every African American from the South through mass migration was an impossibility, Thompson felt that African Americans had to explore other alternatives. Litigation not only gave them a voice in public policy, but it also gave them a means of shaping public opinion in ways that would support an extension of civil rights.

The publication of *The Courts and the Negro Separate School* presaged a flurry of civil rights litigation that significantly altered US law. The NAACP Legal Defense and Educational Fund, Inc., litigation campaign made headway after 1935 in equalizing African American teachers' salaries. Its lawyers argued higher education cases all the way to the Supreme Court and succeeded in preventing the segregated states from providing graduate and professional educational opportunities to Southern whites while denying those opportunities to African Americans in the South. In the space of twenty years, a series of legal victories had declared racial discrimination in housing, voting, teachers' salaries, interstate travel, education, and higher education to be illegal. As a result, more African Americans had access to educational and other opportunities in 1953 than they had in 1935.

It must be noted that in 1935 few people, including Thompson, imagined that the Supreme Court would be prepared to decide the constitutionality of racially segregated public education within their lifetimes. However, on December 9, 10, and 11, 1952, the Supreme Court indeed blasted such beliefs when it heard oral arguments on five cases directly attacking this issue, and one year later, the Court further surpassed these expectations when on December 7, 8, and 9, 1953, it heard oral arguments on "the question of whether legally enforced-segregated public schools violated the constitutional rights of [African Americans] under the 'equal protection' and 'due process' clauses of the 14th and 5th Amendments, respectively."[10] In both instances, the issue was represented by "five cases from Kansas, Delaware, Virginia, South Carolina, and the District of Columbia" that had been consolidated as *Brown v. Board of Education of Topeka*.[11]

When the Court planned to hear the first round of oral arguments related to compulsory segregation in schools, Thompson took the rare step of making his personal feelings public: in his winter 1953 editorial, "The Supreme Court Examines Separate but Equal Schools," he paid tribute to the dedicated service rendered by Charles Hamilton Houston by noting:

> Before venturing to comment on these cases, I would like to say that I have only two personal regrets. The first is that the late Charles H. Houston, who was the father of the movement to have legally-enforced segregated schools outlawed, [did not live to see] this momentous occasion. This regret is somewhat mitigated by the fact that one of his most apt and inspired disciples [Thurgood Marshall], who is giving the best years of his life to carry on this crusade which Charles Houston started, was not only present, but spearheaded the attack in the state cases.[12]

Thompson's second comment applied with equal force when the Court heard the original arguments in December 1952 as well as the reargument of the *Segregated School Cases* in December 1953: as "poor compensation for not being able to be present in person" on either occasion, in December 1952 he "read all the briefs of the appellees and appellants, including the *amicus curiae* brief of the US Government, and . . . the news stories and editorials in three or four papers; listened to all the news reports and comments [he] could get on the radio."[13] A year later, in early December 1953, he again consoled himself by reading "the briefs submitted in these cases—all 1,595 pages of them; and . . . a transcript of the oral argument presented—around some 500 double-spaced, typewritten pages."[14]

In December 1952, because of the implications of the *School Segregation Cases* cases for US foreign policy Thompson believed that the Supreme Court would find it difficult to avoid ruling on the constitutionality of racially segregated public schooling. Moreover, he also thought that

> the Court now has the crucial task of saying whether legally-enforced segregation based solely on race is consonant with the precepts of the democratic way of life which the Constitution proclaims, and which we hold up as a pattern for other nations to follow. The answer to this question is crucial not only for the eight or ten million Negroes immediately affected, but is equally decisive for America herself. And for obvious reasons, as the U. S. State Department and numerous national, civic, and religious organizations have made emphatically clear in many instances in recent years.[15]

Between December 1952 and December 1953, Thompson detected signs that a policy window had opened that would possibly permit significant advances in African Americans' civil rights, and that "the moral atmosphere and climate of world opinion [were] more favorable than in any period since Reconstruction."[16] Yet he also feared that through their inaction, African Americans and their allies would put at risk an opportunity for which so many had fought, and sometimes died, to obtain. Therefore, rather than waiting idly for the Court to decide, Thompson thought it "much more profitable . . . to examine alternatives and to formulate a program for future action. For it is obvious that we have just begun our fight, whether the Court outlaws segregation or whether it merely affirms *Plessy*."[17]

Thompson pointed out that the "Board of Education of the District of Columbia . . . and the white [Parent-Teachers Association]" had recently scheduled hearings to discuss school desegregation, an initiative that he thought it important for "the NAACP, Urban League, Elks (Civil Liberties and Education Departments), National Congress of PTA's, and other national organizations" to join. Moreover, "since the NAACP has spearheaded this movement," Thompson called upon this organization to publicize the hearings [while asking] its state branches [to lead] such conferences," convinced that timely action would allow activists to redouble their efforts while preparing African Americans for any letdowns that might accompany a negative Court decision.[18]

The "wait and see" posture taken by civil rights leaders in 1953 represented a continuation of the stance they had assumed in 1952, doing little to allay Thompson's fears. Indeed, he had increased his apprehensions that progressives were slowly ceding the initiative to the opposition. He had misgivings about "the lack of sufficient constructive planning, either on the part of whites or Negroes, in the event that segregation is outlawed."[19] Nonetheless, it was his hope that "if and when such a decision is rendered [that] there may be found enough constructive statesmanship on the part of both whites and Negroes, to effect the transition [to desegregated public education] with the least possible difficulties."[20]

Three months later, Thompson delayed writing his spring 1954 editorial, "After the US Supreme Court Decision—What?" "to the last possible moment" in the event the Court's decision was imminent. According to his interpretation of events, "the majority" of activists had adopted a "wait and see attitude," preferring to do nothing until the Court issued its ruling for fear that any action on their part would provoke a negative ruling. On the other hand, Thompson felt that too few "influential groups" were using the hiatus to plan their next steps. He reported only hearing of "isolated suggestions here and there, [that lacked any] clear or definite objectives." If he were correct in thinking that, "the first six months after the decision is rendered will be the crucial period which will determine its implementation for years to come," then the advantage would belong to those who had prepared. Soon it would be too late to launch the educational and publicity campaigns necessary for building support for school desegregation in the South.[21]

As the spring 1954 issue of the *Journal* went to press, Thompson learned that "the NAACP is planning to have a meeting of representatives of its state chapters as soon as the decision is rendered. The Southern Regional Council is toying with the idea of setting up interracial committees in each of the segregated school states. The Fund for the Advancement of Education plans to release its report [*The Negro and the Schools*] in May; sooner, if the decision is rendered before that time."[22] Creating one unified, democratic system of public education throughout the South would be a major undertaking, and Thompson saw few options other than urging "the leaders of the [previously mentioned] three national and regional organizations [to confer] and discuss what should be done cooperatively" to extend equal educational opportunities to every child.[23]

As Thompson wrote the concluding sentences of his spring 1954 editorial, "After the Supreme Court's Decree—What?," the feeble attempts at equalization had done little to reduce inequality in the segregated states. Although the racially segregated public schools in the region were separate, they had always been unequal and were becoming increasingly so. Desegregation was not a panacea; he felt that it did offer African Americans one of the few tools available to them in 1954 to equalize public education, and few people, including Thompson, anticipated the furor following a favorable Court decision. Thompson finished his spring 1954 editorial, "After the Supreme Court's Decree—What?," in time to meet the publication deadline, and fewer than three miles away from the Howard University campus, in another District of Columbia neighborhood, the Supreme Court was within weeks of announcing its landmark decision in *Brown v. Board of Education of Topeka* (1954).

NOTES

1. Richard Bardolph, *The Negro Vanguard* (New York: Vintage, 1961), 342.
2. Richard Kluger, *Simple Justice* (New York: Vintage, 1977), 168.
3. Charles H. Thompson, "The Educational and Administrative Reorganization of Hampton Institute," *The Journal of Negro Education*, 9, no. 2 (April 1940): 139.
4. Kluger, 168.
5. Ibid.
6. Dr. Rachel Weddington, interview by author, August 12, 1996, New York City.
7. Ibid.
8. Ibid.
9. Benjamin J. Brawley, letter to Thompson, October 12, 1932, School of Education Papers, Moorland-Spingarn Research Center, Howard University Archives, Howard University, Box 1894, *Journal of Negro Education*.
10. Charles H. Thompson, "Editorial Note: The Supreme Court Examines 'Separate but Equal' Schools," *The Journal of Negro Education*, 22, no. 1 (Winter 1953): 1.
11. Thompson, "The Supreme Court Examines 'Separate but Equal' Schools," 1.
12. Ibid., 2.
13. Ibid.
14. Charles H. Thompson, "Editorial Comment: The Impending Court Decision," *The Journal of Negro Education*, 23, no. 1 (Winter 1954): 1.
15. Thompson, "The Supreme Court Examines 'Separate but Equal' Schools," 2–3.
16. Thompson, "The Impending Court Decision," 1.
17. Thompson, "The Supreme Court Examines 'Separate but Equal' Schools," 3.
18. Ibid.
19. Thompson, "The Impending Court Decision," 2.
20. Ibid.
21. Charles H. Thompson, "Editorial Comment: After the Supreme Court Decision—What?" *The Journal of Negro Education*, 23, no. 2 (Spring 1954): 107.
22. Thompson, "After the Supreme Court Decision—What?" 108.
23. Ibid.

ONE

Sensing the Initiative Slipping Away

After his slow, careful work at reaching a consensus, Chief Justice Earl Warren had succeeded on May 15, 1954, when "the justices met at the regular Saturday conference and voiced their approval for the final drafts of *Brown* and *Bolling*. Both were unanimous."[1] At dinner later that evening with Attorney General Herbert Brownell, Warren had intimated that Monday, May 17, 1954, might be a good day for Brownell to be at the Court. The following day, Warren and Justice William O. Douglas went "hiking along the C&O Canal, an old route from Washington out to Maryland that ran along the banks of the Potomac River."[2] Over the weekend, former Secretary of State Dean Acheson also received word and was present at Court on Monday, May 17. According to Jim Newton, Earl Warren's biographer, several of the reporters were still downstairs in the Court's pressroom for nearly an hour after "the justices took the bench at precisely noon," and they hastened to enter the courtroom only after hearing the announcement of the "reading of the segregation decision" at 12:52 PM.[3]

Speaking not only to those assembled, but also to the American public, the Chief Justice cast the opinion in *Brown* in clear, simple language. The opinion was short to encourage newspapers and magazine editors to reprint it in its entirety, according to Newton. The Chief Justice began:

> In each of the cases, minors of the Negro race, through their legal representatives, seek the aid of the courts in obtaining admission to the public schools of their community on a non-segregated basis. In each instance, they had been denied admission to schools attended by white children under laws requiring or permitting segregation according to race. This segregation was alleged to deprive the plaintiffs of the equal protection of the laws under the Fourteenth Amendment.[4]

Subsequently, Warren discussed the history of the Fourteenth Amendment and the establishment of the separate but equal doctrine, before recounting the development of public education in the United States. Then, Warren presented the constitutional question and the Court's response: "does segregation of children in public schools solely on the basis of race, even though the physical facilities and other 'tangible' factors may be equal, deprive the children of the minority group of equal educational opportunities? We believe that it does." Rather than focusing on the foreign policy implications of the decision that concerned someone like Dean Acheson, the Chief Justice emphasized the destructiveness of racial segregation on African American children's social, intellectual, and psychological development. He concluded by noting: "Separate educational facilities are inherently unequal. Therefore, we hold that the plaintiffs and others similarly situated for whom the actions have been brought are, by reason of the segregation complained of, deprived of the equal protection of the laws guaranteed by the Fourteenth Amendment."[5]

Having dispatched the constitutional question, the Court restored "the cases . . . to the docket" for further argument on the question of relief. It invited all the parties to the *Segregated School Cases*, and "the Attorney General of the United States . . . [to participate. It also extended an invitation to] the Attorneys General of the states requiring or permitting segregation in public education . . . to appear as amici curiae upon request to do so by September 15, 1954, and submission of briefs by October 1, 1954."[6]

Although Thompson welcomed the *Brown* decision and considered it "one of the most important rendered by Court since Dred Scott," the sheer breadth of the Court's decision surprised him.[7] He thought that the Court would require the colleges to desegregate first and then the high schools after educators had gained the necessary experience and expertise to make the process go smoothly; then, and only then, would they begin the process at the elementary level. Thompson felt that had the Court authorized such a procedure, the desegregation of public education would have proceeded in a more orderly and predictable fashion: the public would have known what to expect by the time elementary school desegregation was set to begin, and having become accustomed to the process, they might have also become more receptive to it.

On May 17, 1954, the Supreme Court did not offer any guidance about "the difficult social-engineering job of implementation."[8] Nevertheless, Thompson was confident that the experience obtained in the processes of the desegregation of the US armed forces, industry, and public accommodations over the previous twenty-five years had provided lessons that would make the job of merging the dual system of public education into a unitary system more manageable. Two days after the *Brown* decision, on May 19, 1954, "President Eisenhower urged [public] school officials to end the practice of segregation in . . . the nation's capital by fall 1954, [and, thereby] 'serve as a model for the rest of the country.'"[9] One week later, by a vote of six to two, the District of Columbia's Board of Education voted to "begin the desegregation of the capital's public schools in the fall. [They also] voted to outlaw pupil and teacher transfers [based on] race and ended race labeling in school records."[10]

Thompson did not discuss either of these events in his *Journal* editorials. Instead, he preferred to have people closer to the scene—such as Irene Osborne, a leader of the desegregation movement in Washington, DC, or Paul Cooke, an associate professor of English at Miner Teachers College—record their impressions. Thompson remained convinced that too little had been done before the Court's decision to prepare the public to receive it favorably; yet he was hopeful that Americans would comply with not only the letter but also the spirit of the law. After the Court recessed, Thompson spent the summer months watching developments in the South before capturing in print his hypotheses about the best path forward in the new era created by the Supreme Court's unanimous reversal of *Plessy*.

No records of Thompson's thinking during June, July, and August 1954 have survived, but we do know that he delayed writing his next editiorial, "Between Court Decision and Decree," until after September 10, 1954, because he refers to a news account published on that date in the Washington *Post-Times-Herald* in noting that despite his concern that those supporting desegregation were largely unprepared to take advantage of the Court's favorable ruling, reports from the daily newspapers and *Southern School News* gave him reasons for optimism. He cited newspaper accounts that leading Southern white liberals had accepted:

> the [*Brown*] decision . . . with a reasonable amount of poise and common sense and had encouraged others in the region to do the same, while communities [had started the desegregation process within months of the Court's decision] . . . without serious incident. . . . The early leaders of these desegregation efforts included] the school systems of Washington, D.C., Baltimore, parts of Delaware, West Virginia, Missouri, and other border areas, and even one or two towns in Arkansas.[11]

As a consequence, the 1954 school year began with some progress made in desegregating public schools in the Upper South, the border states, and the midwest. But early results suggested that the sociologist Charles S. Johnson was correct in expecting that enforced school desegregation would split the "solid South," making it possible for the desegregation movement to move faster than had been previously anticipated.[12] Thompson welcomed the decision by a federal court to block an effort by the Federation of Citizens Associations, a group that was then active in promoting residential segregation, to stop school desegregation from proceeding in the District of Columbia.[13] He wrote approvingly of the judge's decision to let desegregation begin in the District before the Court had issued its implementation decree, and he expressed the hope that a similar lawsuit in Baltimore, Maryland, would meet the same fate.

Although Thompson recorded his reasons for being optimistic about the early efforts at desegregation, within a few paragraphs he also pointed to more troubling indicators: on the one hand, "the technical ruling of some attorney general or other state official or agency" prevented several communities from desegregating in September 1954; on the other hand, that month was marred by the "ridiculous spectacle" of communities in which the private schools desegregated rapidly while the public schools remained solidly segregated, and some higher education officials justified keeping African American public colleges segregated while opening former white campuses to African American students.[14] If the consequences of such actions were not damaging, Thompson would have regarded with amusement the theatrics of defiance engaged in by Southern politicians whose conduct "bordered on the irresponsible" and came dangerously to harming members of the public. In fact, the Southern states were sorting themselves into categories ranging from passively hostile to "hardcore states" such as Georgia, Louisiana, Mississippi, South Carolina, and Virginia that were vowing to maintain segregated schooling at any cost.

After penning his autumn 1954 editorial, Thompson had reached two conclusions: first, he believed that the "obstructionist activities engaged in by officials and legislators . . . suggest that we are just beginning the fight for non-segregated public schools in many states"; second, he predicted that a continuation of NAACP litigation campaign was "bound to ensue. And one of the issues that will have to be adjudicated early is whether public funds can be used to support private segregated schools, under whatever guise they may be attempted."[15] The remaining three pages of "Between Court Decision and Decree," dealt with the pressures to compel African American teachers in the South to denounce desegregation or to sign oaths pledging to "support segregated schools."[16] There were, "reports . . . of Negro teachers being intimidated by none-too-thinly-veiled threats of loss of jobs" and more repugnantly, attempts "to persuade Negro leaders to acquiesce in 'voluntary segregation' for a *quid pro quo*."[17] Thompson asserted:

> It has been a source of great satisfaction to many of us that the presidents of Negro state colleges have not permitted themselves to be provoked into making a lot of uncritical public statements about the future of their institutions within the framework of the Court's decision.[18]

However, *Southern School News* also published several negative reports. For example, the presidents of two public African American colleges in Texas had engaged in "the type of questionable, if not invalid 'special pleading'" that they hoped would protect their institutions but which could easily backfire and do irreparable damage. Thompson knew the two presidents in question and held them in high regard, and he was disappointed that they had not been forthright. In remarks that would prove to be prescient, he wrote:

> Certainly it is obvious that a more statesmanlike and educationally sound argument could be presented. . . . If a survey were made of the higher educational needs of *all* of the people, white and Negro, in the state of Texas, as well as of other Southern states, including an appraisal of current educational facilities to meet those needs, it would be undoubtedly be discovered that all of the present higher institutions which amount to anything would be needed to meet the needs of *all* of the people; and if they are good enough, white as well as Negro students will attend them.[19]

Equally troubling were the statements reported for two former presidents of Mississippi Negro Teachers Association, one of whom suggested that $115 million in new buildings would eliminate the need for desegregation in Mississippi and the other that segregated schooling in the community was permissible if African Americans received "a good school building, adequately equipped and properly staffed."[20] Their remarks contradicted the vote by the ninety-member delegation, of which they were part, to not only honor the *Brown* decision, but also to request the "appointment of competent Negroes to all state and local policymaking boards, and a revision of all school laws so as to eliminate all reference to race."[21] The governor was reported to have abruptly adjourned this meeting as soon as the delegation's chairperson finished reading their statement.

Although he understood the fears of African American teachers in the South, such a display of disunity among them could sacrifice the gains made possible by the *Brown* decision. Thus, in the closing paragraphs of "Between Court Decision and Decree," Thompson pointed to the need for "some critical collective thinking" about the problems accompanying desegregation.[22] Noting that these problems were too complicated and varied for any individual to solve and that they "may vary in detail from state to state, it is clear that there are certain basic problems common to all of them."[23] To avoid a crisis, he called for "an early conference of representative Negro educators to discuss some of the more important problems posed by the decision, and to suggest basic principles upon which an approach to their solution should be predicated."[24] This call resonated within Afro-America: within weeks of the publication of Thompson's autumn 1954 editorial, such deliberations were scheduled for Hot Springs, Arkansas, under the sponsorship of Phelps Stokes Fund which was then headed by Frederick D. Patterson, one of Thompson's close allies.

NOTES

1. Jim Newton, *Justice for All: Earl Warren and the Nation He Made* (New York: Riverhead Press, 2007), 322.
2. Ibid., 322–23.
3. Ibid., 324.
4. *Brown v. Board of Education of Topeka*, 347 US 483 (1954), accessed September 15, 2017, *https://supreme.justia.com/cases/federal/us/347/483/case.html.*
5. Ibid.
6. Ibid.
7. Charles H. Thompson, "Editorial Comment: Next Steps in Racial Desegregation in Education," *The Journal of Negro Education*, 23, no. 3 (Summer 1954): 201.
8. Ibid., 201.
9. Bettye Collier-Thomas and V. P. Franklin, *My Soul is a Witness: A Chronology of the Civil Rights Era, 1954–1964* (New York: Henry Holt and Company, 1999), 7.
10. Collier-Thomas and Franklin, *My Soul is a Witness*, 8.
11. Charles H. Thompson, "Editorial Comment: Between Court Decision and Decree," *The Journal of Negro Education*, 23, no. 4 (Autumn 1954): 401.
12. Charles H. Thompson, "Between Court Decision and Decree," 401; Charles S. Johnson, "Some Significant Social and Educational Implications of the U. S. Supreme Court's Decision," *The Journal of Negro Education*, 23, no. 3 (Summer 1954): 364.
13. Irene Osborne, "Section B: Desegregation of Washington Schools: The First 60 Days," *The Journal of Negro Education*, 24, no. 1 (Winter 1955): 84. Wendell E. Pritchett, "A National Issue: Segregation in the District of Columbia and the Civil Rights Movement at Mid-Century," (2005). Faculty Scholarship Paper 1226, p. 1328, accessed September 18, 2017, http://scholarship.law.upenn.edu/faculty_scholarship/1226.
14. Thompson, "Between Court Decision and Decree," 402.
15. Ibid., 402–3.
16. Ibid., 403.
17. Ibid.
18. Ibid., 405.
19. Ibid., italics in the original.
20. Ibid., 403.
21. Ibid.
22. Ibid., 405.
23. Ibid.
24. Ibid.

TWO

The Hot Springs Conference and Teacher Welfare

Two weeks after the publication of Thompson's autumn 1954 editorial, "Between Court Decision and Decree," his reasons for optimism faded as pro-segregation demonstrations rocked Milford, Delaware, blocking that small, mostly rural community's modest attempt at school desegregation. A few days later, copycat student protests against desegregation spread to major cities on the east coast that were planning to desegregate before the Supreme Court issued its implementation decree. Students went on strike to express their opposition to desegegation in Baltimore, Maryland, and a few days later in Washington, DC. The occurrence of strikes in such places, where school desegregation had been expected to be uneventful, underscored the need for "an early conference of representative Negro educators" such as that which Thompson had requested, and when the resistance to desegregation stiffened in the mid-Atlantic states, it became increasingly evident that African American educators needed to arrive at some "basic principles" or standard operating procedures for dealing with the challenges that lay in the unchartered territory subsumed under the terms "desegregation," "non-segregation," or "integration."[1]

Thompson's call resonated far beyond the Howard University campus. Then under the leadership of Frederick D. Patterson, the retired president of Tuskegee Institute and a longtime supporter of Thompson's, the Phelps Stokes Fund's involvement in African American education had begun with its founding in 1911. The Phelps Stokes Fund supported the participation of representatives from the upper Southern states such as Maryland and Virginia, border states such as Kentucky and Tennessee, and Deep Southern states such as Alabama, Florida, Georgia, Louisiana, Mississippi, North Carolina, and South Carolina, as well as representatives from school systems in Western states that were practicing segregation—such as Arkansas, Oklahoma, and Texas. Delaware and Missouri did not send any representatives, nor did West Virginia, the state that soon would close financially struggling Storer College, one of its three publicly supported African American colleges. The largest delegation comprised nine members from North Carolina, which was the location of twelve African American colleges or historically black colleges and universities, including five publicly supported African American colleges. The second-largest delegation came from Texas with seven members, whereas the delegations from Arkansas, Georgia, Mississippi, and Tennessee sent five people each. Eight states and the District of Columbia sent two- or three-person delegations, but only one person represented the African American teachers in Oklahoma. Thompson's October 1954 editorial had been critical of the comments attributed to the presidents of two public historically black colleges and universities in Texas (Prairie View State University and Texas Southern University) that seemed to condone voluntary segregation. It was noteworthy that these two institutions were not represented at the conference, although a consultant affiliated with Prairie View State University did participate.[2]

A remarkably large number of African American Teachers' Associations sent representatives to the conference: they included representatives from the Arkansas Teachers' Association, Colored State Teachers' Association (Texas), Florida Teachers' Association, Kentucky Teachers' Association, Louisiana Education Association, Maryland Educational Association, Mississippi Teachers' Association, North Carolina Negro Teachers' Association, and the Palmetto State Teachers' Association (South Carolina). Several participants affiliated with the Association of Colleges and Secondary Schools for Negroes, an African American accreditation agency, the South Carolina Educational Finance Commission, and the United Negro College Fund attended the meeting, their presence suggesting that in addition to dealing with the problems related to school desegregation, the meeting offered opportunities for problem-solving related to accreditation, changes in teacher licensure requirements, school equalization campaigns, and higher education financing. Five of the *Journal*'s advisory and contributing editors also attended the conference. Two were from North Carolina: J. W. Seabrook, president of Fayetteville State Teachers College, and H. L. Trigg, president of St. Augustine's College. Another two were from Georgia: Rufus E. Clement, president of Atlanta University, and Benjamin E. Mays, president of Morehouse College. And Charles S. Johnson, president of Fisk University, represented African American higher education in Tennessee. Johnson's attendance was significant because he was the most celebrated African American sociologist, and he had served as a successful entrepreneur of education during the era of segregation, his leadership and networking skills outranking Thompson's in most people's estimation.[3]

Although Thompson identified African American teachers and "Negro college presidents—particularly state college presidents" among the educators vulnerable to attacks from the opponents of desegregation, more than 70 percent of the educators in attendance were African American college presidents, vice-presidents, deans, or trustees; in fact, twelve were from African American public colleges, seven of them representing public institutions located in North Carolina, Texas, Alabama, Louisiana, and Missisippi, the last three having been sites of some of the most violent opposition to desegregation.[4] Ten of the fifty-eight educators (more than 17 percent) were leaders of African American teachers' associations who, in addition to their concern for African American teachers' welfare, had firsthand knowledge about the pressures those teachers faced as well as the depth of their commitment to civil rights.[5]

The presence of these educators raised the question of African American teachers' opinions about public school desegregation shortly before the Supreme Court declared segregated public schooling illegal. Research based on "150 Negro public school teachers enrolled in the Graduate School of the State A. and M. College at Orangeburg, South Carolina, during the 1953 Summer Session" captured some of these apprehensions.[6] The researchers, Hurley H. Doddy and G. Franklin Edwards, two Howard University faculty members, addressed an important gap in the contemporaneous literature by designing their study in response to Thompson's spring 1953 editorial, "The Negro Teacher and Desegregation of the Public Schools." Thompson had suggested that tenure laws, the shortage of teachers, and the continued expansion of the student population would operate to make it "practically impossible" for the Southern states "to replace Negro teachers with whites."[7] Doddy and Franklin cautioned against using their findings to draw unwarranted "conclusions [or] inferences [about] . . . the total Negro teacher population of the State [or African American teachers in the Deep South in 1953]."[8] They also pointed out the significant difference between their sample and the number of African American teachers in South Carolina. For example, their sample had 20 percent fewer elementary teachers, 23 percent more secondary teachers, and nearly 18 percent more males than was true of African American teachers in South Carolina in 1953, but despite those limitations, Doddy and Franklin's research provided some data about African American teacher/leaders' opinions on school desegregation. Equally important, it highlighted the resourcefulness and commitment of African American teachers to their profession as well as the working conditions that many of them had experienced on the eve of desegregation.

Statistically, the teachers who responded to the survey: "ranged in age from 25 to 60 years, with a mean age of 34 years," and comprised "104 females and 46 males." "Ninety-five, or 63.3 percent, were elementary school teachers and the remaining 55 taught on the secondary level."

Most "of the 150 [participants] . . . were classroom teachers (110), while 40 [were] principals." According to Doddy and Edwards, "[Their] teaching experience [ranged] from one to thirty-three years, with 85 per cent of the group having five or more years in service."[9] Moreover, "They came from communities [ranging] in size from 100 to more than 60,000 in population." A total of 126 of the respondents provided information on the size of their community, and of those, "approximately 92 percent were from communities of less than 10,000 in population; [while] 41 percent of this group came from areas under 2,500 in population."[10] Doddy and Edwards concluded that most of their participants lived in small communities and worked in schools that had not been chosen for consolidation.[11] The researchers used a questionnaire that sought to obtain information regarding the teachers' attitudes about the likely effect of desegregation respectively on their job security, prospects for promotion, and relationships with white school officials and supervisors.

Most of respondents were "somewhat fearful" that as a consequence of desegregation many African American teachers would lose their jobs and the majority believed that South Carolina might abandon public education before desegregating it, fearing that if the public schools desegregated, white school officials would find ways to "evade granting [them] actual equality in employment, pay, and other benefits."[12] In fact, many reported that relationships with their supervisors had deteriorated since the National Association for the Advancement of Colored People Legal Defense and Educational Fund, Inc. (NAACP-LDF), attack on the constitutionality of segregated public education. Moreover, they also thought that after an end to the segregated system that African Americans would lose the modest roles in policymaking they had once enjoyed, and that accountable only to the white electorate, school officials would give little attention to African American students and teachers' needs. Few respondents anticipated major changes in the years immediately following desegregation, yet nearly two-thirds felt that their prospects for employment would worsen as time passed, and they were also apprehensive that desegregation would result in the closing of small schools such as those in which many of them worked. Many realized that the consolidation of school districts was largely responsible for their predicament and yet they blamed their anticipated job losses on desegregation.

Doddy and Edwards' research also shed light on how African American teachers in small communities barely made a living wage in 1953 despite salary equalization efforts:

> In a number of schools in South Carolina, particularly those located in the small towns and rural areas, many couples are employed in the same school system. In a large number of instances these couples work in the same school. [To understand the apprehensions of such teachers, it is important to understand] two factors now at work in the State. First, in the past several years the consolidation movement has been

> pushed very fast. As a result of this program many small schools have been eliminated. Secondly, there has been a movement in some of the larger cities to separate couples who are teaching in the same building. With an experiential background rooted in these developments, the respondents have come to fear that the process of desegregation will bring with it a reduction in the teaching force. Even if the group were inclined to be optimistic regarding the fact that reductions in teaching personnel will not be entailed, there is the threat that the process will result in marked shifts in personnel, so that many of the couples now teaching in the same schools will be affected.[13]

Doddy and Edwards thought that "Although . . . the enlargement of the consolidation program may be responsible for the untoward conditions which many of the respondents envision, it is not easy for them to separate the influence of these forces from any contribution which might be made by desegregation."[14] Outside the major cities, "few of the Southern states [had] well-defined tenure laws protecting teachers' rights of employment."[15] Sensing that they were vulnerable, many of the teachers pursued graduate study in summer 1953 in the hope that more training might protect them from dismissals or layoffs.

Nearly half of the teachers (49.3 percent) reported a preference for continuing their employment in a segregated school system, adding that as many as 75 percent of their peers held similar if not stronger views.[16] Doddy and Franklin were careful not to confuse the teachers' preference for working in a segregated system with evidence that they preferred racial segregation. Instead, they asked "inasmuch as it is a fact that a segregated school system means inferior schools for Negroes—(and this is the case in South Carolina)—how does one explain the large percentage of Negro teachers who express a preference for that system?" They ruled out "the familiar explanation of 'vested interests' in the present system" because it did not capture fully the dilemma with which the teachers wrestled. Many of the teachers admitted to honestly thinking that "the maintenance of their jobs and the improvement of their economic status [would] best be achieved through the present system."[17] However, the depth and strength of these teachers' (and many African Americans') commitment to civil rights and desegregation were largely unknown variables in summer 1953, according to Doddy and Edwards. Rather, in their view:

> there has not been any systematic investigation of the extent to which large segments of [African Americans] are willing to undergo hardships and personal sacrifices in order that the objectives [of the civil rights movement] might be achieved. It should also be remembered that the ideology of the desegregation movement has been shaped mainly by Negro middle class leaders and by whites of similar persuasion. It is this group which initially has the strongest convictions re-

garding the sanctity of the ends sought and envisions the need of personal sacrifices.[18]

In the autumn of 1954, African American higher education still revolved around teacher training like earth circling the sun. Therefore, threats to African American teachers' job security also threatened the survival of the African American colleges and universities that they had attended. Because so few professional opportunities beyond teaching were available to African Americans in the South, and the support of these teachers was necessary for desegregation to succeed, the seriousness of the October 1954 Conference of Southern Negro Educators in Hot Springs, Arkansas, was thus underscored.

Scheduling the conference on a Tuesday and Wednesday (October 26–27, 1954) probably made it easier for executives at the Phelps Stokes Fund to secure acccommodations for sixty-two people, and most important, to provide a congenial atmosphere for candid discussions. Since the turn of the twentieth century, public accommodations had been racially segregated in Hot Springs, Arkansas, and yet it was a popular destination for conferences or conventions sponsored by African American religious demonimiminations, educational associations, and fraternal orders. For African Americans visiting Hot Springs in 1954, housing would have been available at the homes of friends or in private residences or boarding houses owned by African Americans. They could also obtain lodging in two hotels and spas owned by African Americans: the four-story Pythian Bathhouse and Sanitarium, and the more elegant and spacious Woodman of the Union Building, which then operated under the auspices of the National Baptist Convention. The Woodman of the Union Building was particularly desirable because it:

> featured first-class hotel accommodations . . . a 2,000-seat theater, along with a 600 capacity meeting auditorium, gymnasium, print shop, beauty parlor, and newsstand. Count Basie, Pegleg Bates, and Joe Louis were only a few of the top name entertainers, sports celebrities and political figures who came during its prime.[19]

The Woodman of the Union Building also featured "shops at ground level, a bathhouse, . . . a 75-room hotel, a 100-bed hospital and a nurses' training school, a bank . . . and the organization's executive offices."[20]

The meeting, billed as the Conference of Southern Negro Educators, convened on October 26 and after two days of deliberations it adjourned on October 27, 1954. The participants officially set out to develop some general principles for promoting equal educational opportunity regardless of race while safeguarding the job security of African American teachers in the Southern states, and in a statement co-authored by Benjamin E. Mays and Thompson, they gave a ringing endorsement to the *Brown* decision, and depicted it "as another significant milestone in the nation's quest for a democratic way of life and the Negro's long struggle to become a first-class citizen."[21] The Supreme Court's decision was defined as a "right and moral thing to do" rather than a radical departure from tradition, and the conference urged Southern whites to accept this decision as "a next logical and inevitable step" in the development of the American democracy. The reforms stipulated in *Brown* also "dramatically distinguished" the American way of life from life in "Nazi Germany and Communist Russia."[22]

The conferees professed their faith in the US Constitution, incremental reform, and "the ideal of human brotherhood," and took pride in the fact that "every individual and organizational effort we have made to achieve complete citizenship rights in American life has been within the legal framework of the Federal Constitution."[23]

Aware that failure to honor the principles of legal equality enunciated in *Brown I* might push the emerging nations in Asia and Africa into the orbit of the Union of Soviet Socialist Republics, the conferees appealed to Southern whites' "sense of fair play" and pointed to Southern towns and cities where desegregation had occurred without incident. They welcomed the support the decision had received from Southern white opinion leaders in the press, pulpit, and civic society, and they encouraged the leaders of Southern higher education, black and white, to lead by example by accepting all qualified candidates for admission regardless of race.[24]

Roughly the first half of the conference statement explained how the *Brown* decision served the interests of the South, and it urged Southern white moderates, liberals, and progressives to display the type of leadership, decisiveness, and conviction needed to persuade their compatriots to obey the law. It was the conferees' fear that Southern whites' "preoccupation with the co-educational implication of the decision" might prevent them from grasping the opportunities that desegregation made possible for upgrading public education in the South to the point where every child in the region could reach her or his potential. To that end, the educators "strongly [endorsed] and [pledged their support for] federal aid to education in order that the per capita expenditure in the South may be brought up to a high national average."[25] Having expressly offered their goodwill, the conferees devoted the second half of the statement to articulating a vision of the full and equal citizenship that the *Brown* decision made possible in a South that Edwin Embree, past president of the Julius Rosenwald Fund, had previously characterized as "half Nazi and half democratic."

As believers in the liberating possibilities of education, the educators emphasized

that merging the dual system into one would provide an opportunity to maximize "educational resources." Nonetheless, they expressed their concerns about Southern whites' habit of excluding African Americans, except for a few hand-chosen or "key Negroes" from the councils involved in policymaking and decision-making. The conferees also underscored their belief in shared governance, noting[26]:

> The idea is still too prevalent that the issues involved can be resolved without Negro participation. Some public officials speak as if only white Americans are involved. We are all, Negro and white, deeply and equally involved. Many Negroes can contribute sound, intelligent and statesmanlike techniques for the handling of the inevitable issues. Negroes are able and willing to serve on boards of education, on other policymaking bodies and in administrative capacities throughout the South. They are anxious to share the responsibilities which in too many instances have been monopolized by one segment of the population.[27]

They condemned the efforts by "some leaders and some school officials to intimidate Negro teachers and other citizens under threat of loss of jobs if they expressed approval of the Court's decision" or refused to swear oaths in support of "voluntary segregation."[28] They further warned African American teachers against being manipulated into supporting voluntary segregation schemes, arguing that such actions would not guarantee job security or persuade legislators and reluctant taxpayers to raise the millions of dollars necessary to equalize African American public education.[29] They concluded that the destruction of "the very fabric of our Constitutional Government" was the consequence that reactionary teachers would reap, in addition to the contempt of those officials with whom they had colluded to undermine the *Brown* decision. They reminded their audience that African American and white children had played together in the South since time immemorial, and strongly condemning the "adults who [incited] students to riot or [encouraged] them to" protest, demonstrate, and engage in criminal mischief to prevent students of color from entering school.[30]

Echoing an approach that the lawyers for the NAACP-LDF would advocate in *Brown II* (1955), the educators urged all Southerners of good will to begin the process of public school desegregation immediately. Whereas they recognized that this process would vary in difficulty as well as the amount of time required for accomplishing it, they encouraged officials in every affected school system to partner with African American educators and families and engage in constructive planning.[31] Understanding that some might seek to use planning as a tool for postponing public school desegregation indefinitely, the conferees insisted that all planning proceeded in good faith with the goal of implementing rather than thwarting the decision.[32]

Having personally experienced the sting of racism, the educators deemed segregation a scourge whose undoing through desegregation would allow society to recover gradually from the damage and fears that segregation had inflicted by virtue of living peacefully in an equalitarian society.[33] After arranging to send a press release based on their official statement to "to all major newspapers throughout the country," the conferees disbanded. The leaders were "quite disappointed" when only the *Arkansas Gazette* carried an article related to their meeting in the Friday, October 29, 1954, edition and the *New York Times* belatedly published an article about the conference on November 2, 1954.[34]

In his last published remarks, sociologist Charles S. Johnson confirmed the leaders' disappointment as well as Johnson's high regard for what they had attempted. Perhaps the silence that greeted the news of their accomplishment may have reflected Southern whites' shock that so many educated African Americans in the South voluntarily expressed their preference for desegregation, and an insistence on shared governance that clearly implied that African Americans were capable of self-government. Thus the conference was not a turning point; instead, it marked the beginning of an endurance test. The conferees returned to their homes in fourteen states, and Thompson returned to his home located at 1230 Fairmont Street NW, Washington, DC,[35] armed with a robust list of contacts, several of whom were insiders able to assemble a portrait of the progress or lack of progress in desegregating public education in the South in the years ahead.

NOTES

1. Charles H. Thompson, "Editorial Comment: Between Court Decision and Decree," *The Journal of Negro Education*, 23, no. 4 (Autumn 1954): 405.
2. George Breathett, "Black Educators and the United States Supreme Court Decision of May 17, 1954 (*Brown versus the Board of Education*)," *The Journal of Negro History*, 68, no. 2 (Spring 1983): 205–8.
3. Ibid.
4. Thompson, "Between Court Decision and Decree," 405.
5. Breathett, 205–8.
6. Hurley H. Doddy and G. Franklin Edwards, "Apprehensions of Negro Teachers Concerning Desegregation in South Carolina," *The Journal of Negro Education*, 24, no. 1 (Winter 1955): 26.
7. Charles H. Thompson, "Editorial Comment: The Negro Teacher and Desegregation of the Public Schools," *The Journal of Negro Education*, 22, no. 2 (Spring 1953): 95–101.
8. Doddy and Edwards, 28.
9. Doddy and Edwards, 27.
10. Ibid.
11. Ibid.
12. Ibid., 29.
13. Ibid.
14. Ibid.
15. Ibid., 28.
16. Ibid., 37–38.
17. Ibid., 38.
18. Ibid., 40.
19. National Park Service, US Department of the Interior, "African Americans and the Hot Springs Baths," Hot Springs National Park, Arkansas, 2, accessed September

20, 2017, https://www.nps.gov/hosp/learn/historyculture/upload/african_americans.pdf.

20. Karen Kingsley, "Historic Woodmen of Union Building" [Hot Springs, Arkansas], *SAH Archipedia*, edited by Gabrielle Esperdy and Karen Kingsley, Charlottesville: UVaP, 2012, accessed July 23, 2018,http://sah-archipedia.org/buildings/AR-01-051-0001.

21. Breathett, 202.

22. Ibid.

23. Ibid., 202–3.

24. Ibid., 203.

25. Ibid., 204.

26. Ibid., 204.

27. Ibid.

28. Ibid., 203; according to John W. Davis, Thurgood Marshall anticipated the need for the NAACP to establish a Department of Teacher Protection and Security as early as May 24, 1954. This unit became operational in the NAACP-LDF in January 1955, three months after the Conference of Southern Negro Educators. Please see John W. Davis, "Protecting the Negro Teacher," *The Journal of Negro Education*, 25, no. 2 (Spring 1956): 182.

29. Ibid.

30. Ibid., 204.

31. Ibid.

32. Ibid.

33. Ibid., 205.

34. Ibid., 201; Collier-Thomas and Franklin, *My Soul is a Witness*, 15.

35. Charles H. Thompson, "Questionnaire for Who's Who in American Education," February 13, 1959, School of Education Papers, Moorland-Spingarn Research Center, Howard University Archives, Howard University, Box 1894, *Journal of Negro Education*; Thompson resided at this address as early as April 27, 1942, according to the World War II draft registration card that Thompson signed on April 27, 1942: see Ancestry.com. *U.S., World War II Draft Registration Cards, 1942* [database online]. Lehi, UT: Ancestry.com Operations, Inc., 2010; Original data: US Selective Service System. *Selective Service Registration Cards, World War II: Fourth Registration*. Records of the Selective Service System, Record Group Number 147. National Archives and Records Administration.

THREE

Litigation as a Twin of Direct Action

When Thompson composed the opening paragraphs of his winter 1955 editorial, "Recent Briefs Submitted in the Segregation Cases," few people apart from the lawyers of the National Association for the Advancement of Colored People Legal Defense and Educational Fund, Inc. (NAACP-LDF), or the Attorneys General in the affected states and their advisers could match his expertise. The Court had ruled that segregated public education was inherently discriminatory, and then the legal fight was shifting to the processes whereby the Court would define and administer relief. In *Brown I*, Chief Justice Warren had recognized the magnitude of the problem of ridding *de jure* racial segregation from US public education stemming from not only the scope of the decision that affected more than six million students but also the need to tailor relief to local conditions.[1]

Therefore, the Court ordered further argument to decide whether desegregation should proceed immediately or if "this Court, in the exercise of its equity powers, [should] permit an effective gradual adjustment to be brought about from existing segregated systems to a system not based on color distinctions?"[2] In addition, the Court ordered further argument to decide what the decrees for relief should entail and to outline the procedures for ensuring the various states' compliance. In *Brown II*, the Chief Justice had limited participation to those parties with an immediate stake in the answers to the questions it had posed (i.e., the NAACP-LDF on behalf of the plaintiffs, Delaware, the District of Columbia, Kansas, South Carolina, and Virginia [the defendants in the instant cases], and the Attorney General of the United States). He also invited "The Attorneys General of the states requiring or permitting segregation in public education . . . to appear as amici curiae."[3] Subsequently, "the parties, the United States, and the States of Florida, North Carolina, Arkansas, Oklahoma,

Maryland, and Texas filed briefs and participated in the oral argument" leading to *Brown II*.[4] In doing so, he created a situation pitting a small voluntary association against an increasingly unified and defiant South.

Facing the legal and material resources assembled by Arkansas, Delaware, the District of Columbia, Florida, Kansas, Maryland, North Carolina, Oklahoma, South Carolina, Texas, and Virginia, the NAACP-LDF was at a disadvantage. The resources and prestige of the Southern states were heavily invested in maintaining a position counter to the Court's ruling in *Brown I*. Nonetheless, Robert L. Carter, George E. C. Haynes, Thurgood Marshall, James M. Nabrit Jr., Louis L. Redding, and Spotswood Robinson III, were competent counsel who had innovated civil rights law and used policy research to extend constitutional guarantees to minority groups. Marshall also turned to forums such as the NBC radio program "Youth Wants to Know" as well as the black press to keep the public informed with a view of shaping public opinion in support of the NAACP's position.[5]

Thompson's editorial focused on the differences in the briefs and identified three distinct approaches. He compared the brief of the Attorney General of Florida that illustrated the perspective of the segregated states against those submitted by NAACP-LDF and the US Attorney General. His analysis demonstrated that US Attorney General Herbert Brownell occupied a middle ground, siding with the Florida brief on some issues and with the NAACP-LDF on others: Florida and Brownell favored a gradual approach to desegregation, whereas the NAACP-LDF wanted desegregation to begin immediately. For the latter, Thurgood Marshall echoed the belief that the ninety-one years since 1863 which African Americans had waited for equality constituted all the gradualism that the Court should expect them to countenance. Moreover, the NAACP-LDF brief required the affected states to file periodic progress reports and requested the Supreme Court to set a firm date for those states to complete the process of desegregating public education. In the winter of 1955, Thompson pointed to the discrepancies between the federal government's position and that of the NAACP-LDF on the scale and pace of desegregation by noting "The Government brief and the brief of the Attorney General of Florida [were] based upon exactly the opposite assumption from that upon which the NAACP brief [was] based."[6]

On the other hand, the NAACP-LDF and the US Attorney General were in agreement that not only was desegregation legally binding but that the Southern states had to demonstrate their "good faith" by desegregating public education as rapidly as the resolution of "prerequisite administrative and mechanical procedures" would allow (*Brown II*).[7] Despite agreeing with the government's position on certain key points, the Florida brief occupied its own philosophical and ideological space and sought to have the local courts retain jurisdiction of the cases. Florida's formula for relief would undermine the effectiveness of *Brown I* as a class action by requiring African Americans to engage in additional litigation to gain admission to formerly white schools in their communities. The Florida brief resonated with the same type of logic and determination that had sustained Jim Crow practices for nearly a century: African American freedom represented a potent threat to the social order and, therefore, had to be tightly controlled. Florida would reinvent the rules of due process by barring African Americans from entering any previously all-white school unless they could document their compliance with every stipulation in a complicated admission and appeals process that included a mandatory appeal to the state Board of Education. African American students had to complete those requirements before they could pursue other remedies, and failure to do so would render null and void their claims of discrimination. In effect, Florida would shift the burden of proof from the states onto African American students and their families. Although the tone of the Florida brief was academic and polite, it left little doubt that the state's leaders would use every means at their disposal to ensure that the desegregation of public education in that state proceeded at a snail's pace, if at all. Thompson concluded his winter 1955 editorial by asking his readers to imagine themselves dealing with the issues before the Court. He wrote, "It will be interesting to speculate meanwhile what we would do and why, if we were the Court. This little feat of mental gymnastics will make us more sympathetic with whatever decree the Court may render."[8]

In the winter of 1955, the depth and strength of African Americans' commitment to the civil rights struggle remained unknown, but as thermometers in the nation's capital reported falling temperatures, race relations had reached the boiling point south of the Mason-Dixon Line. In Mississippi, for example, White Citizens' Councils orchestrated a boycott against African American business owners and professionals who supported the civil rights struggle. The White Citizens' Councils targeted the very group that Thompson and the other educators meeting at Hot Springs had called upon to lead the desegregation effort in the Deep South, in keeping with the theory that these people should be less vulnerable to economic reprisals than African American teachers. However, as Newton had observed, "For every action, there is an equal and opposite reaction," and the White Citizens' Councils boycott prompted a counter-boycott by the members of Mississippi chapter of the NAACP. In a December 9, 1954, meeting in Jackson, Mississippi, they "called for an all-out boycott of products and services," of any company or executive that used "threats and intimidation" to derail African American progress.[9]

A week later, on December 18, the *New York Times* reported another development of which Thompson was undoubtedly aware: the NAACP opened a new department to "protect Negro teachers, principals, and administrative personnel" against the loss of jobs resulting from desegregation. It chose "Dr. John W. Davis, former president of West Virginia

State College and director of US Foreign Operations Administration in Liberia," as the first director.[10] Subsequently, the NAACP launched a fundraising drive to create a "30 million dollar war chest to support Southern blacks active in civil rights campaigns" that had been "threatened [with] loss of home mortgages"; these developments were as reliable a herald of things to come as was the approval by the white voters in Mississippi by "a 2 to 1 margin . . . [of] a constitutional amendment to abolish the public schools and subsidize private schools in order to maintain segregated education."[11] Rather than splitting the South, the desegregation of public education seemed ready to harden segregation while unifying its proponents. It remained an open question whether this resistance among Southern whites would prompt a stronger reaction among African Americans. Would the strength of middle-class African Americans and their white allies' commitment to civil rights remain high? Was there considerably more support for civil rights in the African American grassroots than sympathetic scholars had realized? In the winter of 1955, Thompson gave no indication that he had formulated answers or hypotheses concerning such questions.

Thompson did not voice an opinion until March 28, 1955, shortly after the US Senate had confirmed John Marshall Harlan, II, as an associate justice of the Supreme Court, to fill the position opened by the death of Robert Houghwout Jackson from a heart attack on October 9, 1954. In "Some Significant Byproducts of the May 17th Decision," Thompson's spring 1955 editorial, he informed the *Journal*'s readers that the Court had scheduled oral argument in the *School Segregation Cases* for April 11, 1955, shortly after the Senate's confirmation of Justice Harlan. By the time the spring issue was in print, Thompson believed that "oral argument will be over," and that the Court might announce the terms of relief before its summer recess.[12]

Thompson also reported that "Congressional Committees on education" recently had held hearings on "a bill authorizing government aid in construction of much-needed school buildings."[13] The Hot Springs conference press release had supported increased federal aid to education to address the problems involved with desegregating public education, the support of the conferees being offered on the condition that such funding be distributed equitably and without a smidgen of discrimination. Accordingly, Thompson added that some had asked whether the states maintaining segregation should be ineligible for such federal funding and if that ban should be part of the authorizing legislation.[14]

As early as 1937, the policy community supporting federal aid to education had split over this question; some believed that adding non-discriminatory language or enforcement mechanisms would jeopardize the legislation's chances of passage. In time, their objections became an enduring theme of federal aid to education debates, so it was not surprising that similar reservations surfaced in early 1955, or for Thompson to reject them promptly as morally and intellectually bankrupt. He also encouraged the supporters of non-discriminatory enforcement mechanisms to hold firm against such specious reasoning.[15] He reasserted the principle that he had endorsed in Hot Springs and he had observed throughout his career: a refusal to compromise his principles, however tantalizing the reward. Echoing the educators' meeting at Hot Springs, Thompson discouraged his readers from taking any action that might weaken support for desegregation or the fight for equal rights, for he firmly believed that to do so would jeopardize the larger civil rights struggle and the gains already won at great sacrifice. It would be "too much like winning a war and losing the peace."[16]

Next, Thompson assayed the destructive effects of racial segregation on human development: from birth to the grave, he suggested segregation was intimately bound to a person's sense of identity, sense of purpose, and self-respect. No aspect of life was beyond its reach, not even childhood friendships where blurred racial boundaries hardened into impenetrable barriers in adulthood, as children assumed their designated social roles as superiors and subordinates. During the era of segregation, Thompson wrote: "Throughout the South, public parks have been just as rigidly segregated as the schools; and with similar results. Negroes have usually had set aside for them a token recreation area and have been excluded entirely from all of the facilities set aside for whites. In a few places, the expedient has been devised of setting aside certain days for Negroes and whites, as in the case of some of the golf courses."[17]

In early 1955, Thompson questioned whether the *Brown* decision was limited to public education or whether racial segregation and racial discrimination were illegal in other sectors of US society. "Many of us have wondered," he noted, about how far the courts would apply the principles enunciated in *Brown v. Board of Education*. A decision by the Fourth Circuit Court of Appeals provided "a partial answer," in its decision that "segregation in public parks was just as unconstitutional as in the schools."[18] In early 1955, any breakthrough in the direction of equality, however modest, prompted a reaction from those who were determined to maintain segregation despite its illegality. Virginia was part of the US Court of Appeals for the Fourth Circuit's jurisdiction, as was Baltimore, and immediately upon learning of the ban against racially segregated parks in Baltimore, the NAACP in Virginia filed a lawsuit to desegregate public parks in the Commonwealth of Virginia. Subsequently, Thompson received reports that state officials in Virginia had developed plans in secret to evade the *Brown* decision by leasing the public parks to private individuals. He was confident that the legality of the practice would be challenged in court and predicted that "the question of private operation of state-aided facilities, as is threatened by three or four states in connection with the schools, will be decided on this issue raised by the park situation in Virginia."[19]

From Thompson's perspective, ebb and flow, thrust and parry, and jabbing, feinting, and then counter-punching characterized the desegregation movement and the larger civil rights struggle in the spring of 1955. Nonetheless, just as stones tossed into a pond produce ripples on the water's surface, Thompson believed that the theory of social dynamism, similar to the proposals of Gunnar Myrdal, determined that social phenomena were interrelated, and that a change in one direction stimulated changes in other directions. The endless skirmishing in the early months of desegregation revealed the extent of the resolve, discipline, and resilience that the supporters of desegregation would need to summon if they were to prevail against opponents who freely drew upon the resources of the Southern states. Thompson therefore concluded his editorial with remarks that were part observation and part admonition: "the price of freedom is eternal vigilance and continual striving." African Americans had but one choice: "if we are to have the important May 17th decision implemented, we have got to keep at it. The fight has just begun. May we keep everlastingly at it."[20]

As was often the case, events outpaced the *Journal*'s publication schedule, and by the time Thompson's summer 1955 editorial, "The Desegregation Decision—One Year Afterward," appeared in print, the Supreme Court had issued its implementation ruling, or *Brown II*. Thompson devoted more than half of his four-page editorial to reprinting the Court's decision in full, addressing the predicament of his African American readers in the South, many of whom still had access only to racially segregated libraries that might constrain their ability to receive such information. Thompson published the Court's opinion without commentary, leaving that task to the many contributors to the *Journal*'s 1955 Yearbook. Because he had planned the contents of the 1955 Yearbook before the Court issued its ruling in *Brown II*, Thompson asked each contributor "to make a supplementary statement covering the reaction to this decree, where possible."[21] The Court appeared to have selected elements from the US Attorney General's brief as well as from the legal briefs submitted by the NAACP-LDF and the Attorney General of Florida. Consistent with the position advocated by the NAACP-LDF and the US Justice Department, *Brown II* reiterated the constitutional principle established in *Brown I* noting that: "These cases were decided on May 17, 1954. The opinions of that date, declaring the fundamental principle that racial discrimination in public education is unconstitutional, are incorporated by reference. All provisions of federal, state, or local law requiring or permitting such discrimination must yield to this principle."[22]

The Court rejected the NAACP-LDF's call for desegregation to begin immediately; instead, it opted for desegregation to proceed gradually as recommended by the US Attorney General and the Attorney General of Florida. In doing so, the Court recognized a necessary balance between "the personal interest of the plaintiffs in admission to public schools as soon as practicable on a nondiscriminatory basis" and "the public interest in the elimination of such obstacles [that prevented the plaintiffs' non-discriminatory admission] in a systematic and effective manner."[23] Echoing the recommendations in the US Attorney General, the Attorney General of Florida, and the NAACP-LDF's briefs, the Court chose to return or "remand the cases [to the courts that originally heard them]." Those courts were to take the appropriate legal actions that were "necessary and proper to admit to public schools on a racially non-discriminatory basis with all deliberate speed the parties to these cases."[24]

In recognition of the complexity of desegregating public education systems in seventeen states and the District of Columbia, the Court assigned to school authorities the responsibility for resolving such issues. It tasked the courts with deciding whether those school officials were acting in good faith in desegregating public education as promptly as local circumstances allowed.[25] The Court also ordered the school districts involved in the litigation to begin "a prompt and reasonable start toward full compliance." It cautioned those who might think that obstructionism or violence would nullify its decision by asserting that it would not abandon the constitutional principles involved "because of disagreement with them."[26]

The 1955 issue of the Yearbook consisted of twenty-one chapters, eighteen of which presented case studies assessing the progress or lack of progress toward desegregating public education in the Southern states. The three concluding chapters provided critiques in which the authors reflected on the case studies of desegregation and brought their expertise to bear on the issues those case studies raised. In his concluding chapter, Fisk University sociologist Preston Valien offered an optimistic review of the progress made in desegregating public education in the South in contrast to the more cautionary and nuanced assessment by University of Louisville sociologist C. H. Parrish, who identified the limitations of desegregation as a remedy for discrimination. Robert L. Carter and Thurgood Marshall, two of the attorneys who had developed the strategy, the legal briefs, and the oral arguments resulting in the Supreme Court's landmark *Brown* decisions, contributed the Yearbook's closing chapter. When checking the 1955 Yearbook's table of contents, readers who might have looked forward to reading their account for guidance on advancing desegregation in their local communities would not be disappointed.

The essay by sociologist Preston Valien suggested that he was familiar with an essay contributed to the previous year's Yearbook by sociologist Charles S. Johnson whom Thompson had once saluted as "without doubt the outstanding student of race relations in the" United States."[27] Valien quoted the "apt phrase [and idea] of Charles S. Johnson [that], the desegregation decision has served to accelerate the 'disintegration' of the Solid South," noting his characterization of the *Brown* decision as a "historic ruling, which has been termed more sociological than legal."[28] A Southerner, Valien described the region's reaction to *Brown I* and *II* as ranging from "declarations of unyielding resistance on the one hand" to hurried compliance. He identified Georgia, Louisiana, Mississippi, and South Carolina among the most recalcitrant states that threatened to abolish public education before desegregating it. Midway that range were another group of Southern states had decided to "wait and see" what developments might occur and especially what the implementation decrees would require.[29]

People in the most resistant or "hard core" states had also formed White Citizens' Councils to suppress free speech and dissent by using "economic pressure" to silence or exile anyone who did not fully subscribe to the doctrine of segregation. Valien reported that these states had also "[launched] large-scale public school equalization programs in the hope that Negroes will accept 'voluntary' segregation."[30] With the passage of time, Valien thought, school equalization programs might prove to be their own undoing, and he hoped that these measures would eventually backfire by increasing the support for desegregation among Southern whites when they realized that desegregation provided a way for them to obtain otherwise unthinkable educational opportunities for their children. Despite the heated rhetoric in summer 1955, Valien detected signs that, at least for politicians in the "hard core" states, this defiance was simply a ruse and that they were persisting in order to prolong segregation by testing a variety of delaying tactics in the courts.[31]

Valien's essay also pointed to little noticed, yet important, changes, for example, the existence of some type desegregation in every Southern state including the "hard core," on military bases, in independent schools, and in parochial schools in communities where the desegregation of public education was meeting with resistance. Equally important, although the results of public opinion polls and referenda confirmed that the vast majority of Southern whites preferred to maintain segregation, they also indicated that these citizens would "comply with the law when desegregation is ordered."[32] Public officials had a decisive effect on their community's responses to desegregation; indeed, when these officials' policies were clear, and they made sure that the police swiftly enforced those policies, much of the opposition to desegregation melted away. The gubernatorial campaigns in 1954 had been free of race-baiting, and Valien felt that those elections might signal a "de-emphasis of race in Southern politics," "greater interest in public education," and strengthened democracy in the region. Although the opposition to desegregation in the region tended to foster an "organized counter-resistance," he felt that this development was healthier in the end than the passive acceptance of the status quo.[33]

Carter and Marshall, aged thirty-eight and forty-seven respectively, in 1955 had successfully used the law to combat injustice, and Thompson felt that in making their assessment available to *Journal* readers, he was rendering them a service by providing informed guidance on reaping the maximum value from the Court's recent rulings. Despite the fact that the Court had rejected several of the NAACP-LDF's positions, Carter and Marshall viewed the decree as "about as effective as one could have expected" noting that for the foreseeable future, the "lower courts, and particularly the federal courts, [would serve as] super school boards until desegregation has been accomplished throughout the United States."[34] While the lower courts had considerable latitude in deciding the pace and scope of desegregation, Carter and Marshall reminded readers that *Brown* only had meaning if African Americans filed additional lawsuits. They underscored this point repeatedly: the only way to "end the discriminatory practices" was by grinding down the opposition through subsequent rounds of litigation. They encouraged the *Journal*'s readers "to face the fact that in the Deep South, with rare exceptions, desegregation will become a reality only if Negroes exhibit real militancy and press [relentlessly] for their rights. And this would have been the situation no matter what kind of decision the Court had handed down."[35] Admitting that the Supreme Court's rulings applied only to the litigants in *Brown I* and *Brown II*, they explained that the NAACP had plans for broadening these decisions' reach by:

> [directing] its branches to file petitions with school boards this summer, asking for desegregation, and to commence lawsuits if nothing has been done by the opening of school, September 1955. Where the school board refuses to act, the Negro parents and their children will have to become plaintiffs in lawsuits in federal courts in which they will ask the courts to order the school board to comply with the Supreme Court ruling.[36]

Carter and Marshall anticipated "a flood of litigation" in the ensuing years, and they were also confident that desegregation would become a reality "throughout the United States—tomorrow in some places, the day after in others and many, many moons hence in some, but it will come eventually to all."[37] To hasten that day, they encouraged African Americans and their allies "to get a copy of the opinion, read it and explain its implications to others," and further:

> Efforts should be made to secure the support for voluntary desegregation from among individuals and organizations, and with that support, pressure should be brought on school boards to get them to voluntarily desegregate their schools. Each local NAACP Branch will be engaged in an effort to secure voluntary compliance in many areas in the South and will need and welcome all the assistance it can get.[38]

Segregated schooling was not a regional but a national problem, they explained; therefore, "if segregation in public schools is bad for our children in Atlanta, Georgia, [then] it ought to be equally bad for them in New York City, Chicago, Philadelphia, or Boston."[39] Only by directing "the strongest pressures against the continuation of segregation, North or South . . . [did they believe that it would be possible to eradicate] discrimination in the United States."[40]

In his chapter, C. H. Parrish pinpointed many of the problems that ultimately weakened desegregation as public policy. Rapid, or as he phrased it, "precipitate" desegregation occurred in small communities mainly because of the financial savings that desegregation made possible when school officials hastily closed African American schools and dismissed qualified African American teachers with little warning or forethought, whereas in large cities political calculations deterred school officials from taking similar action. According to insiders such as Irene G. Osborne, "option" plans or features "[allowed students] to stay where enrolled until graduation," Parrish and other critics felt that they proved disastrous from the outset in Washington, DC; Baltimore, Maryland; and "virtually all the desegregated districts of Missouri and West Virginia," and also blamed them for significantly "[holding] back [or slowing] integration."[41]

Using Washington, DC, as an example, Parrish wrote: "In Washington the option is seen as 'the one flaw that tips the scale against the positive accomplishments' . . . [By] the time the option runs out a pattern of evasion and transfer from school zones may have been firmly established."[42] Moreover, in West Virginia, "the option plan has not prevented the closing of Negro schools or the consequent dismissal of Negro teachers."[43] In addition, Parrish believed that the option plan "[shifted] an important educational responsibility from school administrators, who should rightfully accept it, to parents, who are not prepared to assume it."[44] Therefore, he concluded, "a reappraisal of the option principle is called for very soon."[45] Parrish also raised the following objections:

> The tendency to measure the success of a desegregation program in terms of the number or the percentage of Negro children in "integrated" schools is dangerous because it mistakes the beginning of the problem for its solution. There is still inadequate recognition of the fact that no two communities are alike and that what works in one situation may fail to work in another. The unrewarding search for the right formula goes on. The recurring question of what grade it is best to start with often implies a reluctance to start at all.[46]

Parrish's subsequent remarks echoed the results of Doddy and Franklin's research: race relations had deteriorated after the filing of the school segregation cases, and African American teachers reported sensing a change and feeling that relationships with their white supervisors had become chillier, more distant, and adversarial. The setting and climate in which negotiations occur can have a significant effect on the resulting outcomes, as experts in conflict resolution such as Dudley Weeks (1992) have noted. In a similar vein, Parrish pointed out the importance of the leaders of school desegregation efforts being committed to educating all children. Toward the end of his essay, Parrish asserted that "[not] enough attention has been given to the sincerity of purpose of the school administrator as a factor in the success or failure of desegregation plans. The question raised here with respect to desegregation is not 'how much' nor 'how fast,' but 'with what spirit.'"[47]

Thompson reminded his readers that while the courts held center stage, that nothing worth having comes easily, and that if the nation was to gain anything worthwhile from the *Brown* decision, African Americans and their allies had to shake off any initial setbacks. Thus, on the first anniversary of the groundbreaking *Brown* decision, Thompson declared, "The fight has just begun." And, for his part, he pledged and hoped that his words rallied others to "keep everlastingly at it."[48]

NOTES

1. John E. Batchelor, *Race and Education in North Carolina: From Segregation to Desegregation* (Baton Rouge, LA: Louisiana State University Press, 2015), 7.
2. *Brown v. Board of Education of Topeka*, 347 U.S. 483 (1954).
3. Ibid.
4. Ibid.
5. "Thurgood Marshall, guest appearance, 'Youth Wants to Know,'" November 28, 1954, NBC Television, accessed July 23, 2017, https://catalog.loc.gov/vwebv/search?searchCode=LCCN&searchArg=97508717&searchType=1&permalink=y.
6. Charles H. Thompson, "Editorial Comment: Recent Briefs Submitted in the Segregation Cases," *The Journal of Negro Education*, 24, no. 1 (Winter 1955): 2–3.
7. Thompson, "Recent Briefs Submitted in the Segregation Cases," 2.
8. Ibid., 5.
9. Collier-Thomas and Franklin, 16.
10. Ibid., 17.
11. Ibid.
12. Charles H. Thompson, "Editorial Comment: Some Significant Byproducts of the May 17th Decision," *The Journal of Negro Education*, 24, no. 2 (Spring 1955): 91.
13. Thompson, "Some Significant Byproducts of the May 17th Decision," 91.
14. Ibid.
15. Ibid.
16. Ibid.; the phrase, "winning the war and losing the peace" was one that Thompson had often used when describing the disillusionment of progressives in the United States following World War I.
17. Ibid.
18. Ibid., 91–92.
19. Ibid., 92.
20. Ibid.
21. Charles H. Thompson, "Editorial Comment: The Desegregation Decision—One Year Afterward," *The Journal of Negro Education*, 24, no. 3 (Summer 1955): 162.
22. Thompson, "The Desegregation Decision—One Year Afterward," 162.
23. *Brown v. Board of Education of Topeka*, 349 U.S. 294 (1955); Thompson, "The Desegregation Decision—One Year Afterward," 163.
24. *Brown v. Board of Education of Topeka*, 349 U.S. 294 (1955); Thompson, "The Desegregation Decision—One Year Afterward," 164; More specifically: "the special statutory United States District Courts of three judges in the Kansas, South Carolina and Virginia cases, an ordinary United States District Court of one judge in the District of

Columbia case, and the State Supreme Court in the Delaware case." See Robert L. Carter and Thurgood Marshall, "The Meaning and Significance of the Supreme Court Decree on Implementation," *The Journal of Negro Education*, 24, no. 3 (Summer 1955): 397.

25. *Brown v. Board of Education of Topeka*, 349 U.S. 294 (1955); Thompson, "The Desegregation Decision—One Year Afterward," 163.

26. *Brown v. Board of Education of Topeka*, 349 U.S. 294 (1955).

27. Charles H. Thompson, "Editorial Comment: Race Relations in the United States: The Need for Effective Leadership," *The Journal of Negro Education*, 13, no. 1 (Winter 1944): 2.

28. Preston Valien, "The Desegregation Decision—One Year Afterward—A Critical Summary," *The Journal of Negro Education*, 24, no. 3 (Summer 1955): 389–90.

29. Valien, "The Desegregation Decision—One Year Afterward—A Critical Summary," 390.

30. Ibid.

31. Ibid.

32. Ibid., 394.

33. Ibid., 395–96.

34. Robert L. Carter and Thurgood Marshall, "The Meaning and Significance of the Supreme Court Decree on Implementation," *The Journal of Negro Education*, 24, no. 3 (Summer 1955): 397–98.

35. Ibid., 402.

36. Ibid., 401.

37. Ibid., 402–3.

38. Ibid., 403.

39. Ibid., 403–4.

40. Ibid., 404.

41. Irene Osborne and Richard K. Bennett, "Eliminating Educational Segregation in the Nation's Capital, 1951–1955," *The Annals of the American Academy of Political and Social Science, Racial Desegregation and Integration*, 304, (March 1956): 103; C. H. Parrish, "Desegregation in Public Education—A Critical Summary," *The Journal of Negro Education*, 24, no. 3 (Summer 1955): 385–86.

42. Parrish, 385.

43. Ibid.

44. Ibid., 386.

45. Ibid., 385–86.

46. Ibid., 386.

47. Ibid., 387.

48. Thompson, "Some Significant Byproducts of the May 17th Decision," 92.

FOUR

"This Leadership is neither ignorant nor afraid"

In anticipation of the *Journal*'s twentieth[AQ1] anniversary, Thompson had secured the financing to sponsor the groundbreaking, well-attended, and historically significant "Conference on Racial Integration in Education" that was held at Howard University's Rankin Memorial Chapel across the quad from his office in Douglass Hall in April 1952. Now, the situation was different: another important career milestone was approaching for Thompson, the editor. He had begun teaching at Howard University nearly thirty years earlier, and he had previously spent a year working as a supervisor of instruction in the South and another year teaching in a highly regarded high school in the Midwest. As he reflected on the *Journal*'s twenty-fifth year of uninterrupted publication, introspection rather than pride best described the mood of his three-page editorial, "The Twenty-Fifth Volume of the *Journal of Negro Education*."

Around when Thompson was sketching his editorial comments, the front page of the December 6, 1955, Washington *Afro American* reported:

> In the wee hours of Tuesday morning, a group of unidentified white persons [when making their second attack . . . pumped] three shotgun blasts [into the funeral home operated by Billy Fleming, National Association for the Advancement of Colored People (NAACP) member and] nephew of Reverend Mr. [J. A.] DeLaine, an NAACP leader and kingpin in the Clarendon County school segregation suit that led the Supreme Court's desegregation decision. . . . [When attempting to identify his assailants, Billy Fleming had asserted:] "It's one of those things here in Clarendon County, [South Carolina.] The White Citizens' Council is bringing economic and other pressure against members of the NAACP, but it would be hard to single out any one person or group."[1]

Thompson did not dwell on contemporaneous events in his winter 1956 editorial, but he sought to assess not only the *Journal*'s past contributions but also its relevance as the era of *de jure* racial segregation began to fade and that of desegregation seemed a strange mixture of daylight on the one hand and starless night on the other. To ensure that the fog of memory did not distort his recollection, Thompson reread his debut editorial from April 1932 that posed the question, "Why a *Journal of Negro Education*?" He recalled that as a much younger scholar he had founded the *Journal* to fulfill three purposes:

> *first,* to stimulate the collection and facilitate the dissemination of facts about the education of Negroes; *second,* to present discussion involving critical appraisals of proposals and practices relating to the education of Negroes, and *third,* to stimulate and sponsor investigations of problems incident to the education of Negroes.[2]

Evaluating his success was a task that he would leave to the *Journal*'s readers, but he considered that it would be remiss, however, not to point out that a careful review of the magazine's twenty-four volumes "will reveal that there is scarcely a single problem in [African American education] which the *Journal* has not discussed." He also took pride in the fact that "it would be difficult to find a comprehensive study or critical discussion of any problem in this area by other agencies which does not make reference to the *Journal* in some manner."[3] "In fact," he continued, "If we can believe the overwhelming majority of our 'fan mail,' it would appear that the *Journal* has greatly surpassed our original expectations. And yet, [he concluded,] no one is more conscious of its shortcomings than we are."[4]

In an atmosphere where the implications of the Supreme Court's rulings in the *School Segregation Cases* raised questions about the legitimacy of African American organizations, he wondered whether the *Journal*'s "original purpose [was] still valid" and if its name was "still appropriate."[5] Fueling his concerns were the questions from readers and associates about the *Journal*'s purpose and mission now that the era of *de jure* segregation was nearing its end. Rather than sidestep these issues, Thompson approached them as problems worthy of thoughtful analysis. He researched how others who were in a similar situation had dealt with minority status in the United States and found, for example, that:

> despite the fact that Jews are more nearly integrated in the American social order than Negroes, Attwood[6] recently found that there are some 300 national Jewish organizations in the United States today. What is equally important and more pertinent here is the fact that the "Union List of Serials" contains upward of 300 Jewish periodicals, over half of which are published in this country, and a surprising number have little or nothing to do with religion or culture.[7]

Indeed, groups ranging from Japanese Americans to women had elected to follow the path taken by Jewish organizations, including maintaining specialized publications that addressed their specific interests and concerns.

Thompson had dealt with a similar situation in 1934: when a movement was afoot to close every small, African American college in the South that was experiencing financial difficulties. Then, he had insisted on having not only sound evaluation standards in place but also on using those standards for their intended purpose before the powers advocating could close a single college. That crisis had passed without sound standards being developed; decades later, the *Brown* decision revived this issue as well as the temptation to deal with it summarily, still without giving the problem the thoughtful research and analysis that it deserved. According to Thompson, nearly two years after the *Brown* decision, "no one or no group [had] yet developed any well-considered or definite criteria on the basis of which one can determine the continued need for [African American] agencies, nor when and under what circumstances they should be abandoned, or if reoriented, in what direction."[8] As was his standard operating practice, Thompson concluded by asking his readers to share their opinions with the Editorial Board regarding three major questions: should the *Journal* change its name, were its three founding purposes still valid, and did they provide the appropriate philosophical base from which to operate the magazine?[9]

In spring 1956, Thompson detected something "strangely familiar" about the South's response to the *Brown* decision. When measured in terms of what he called "truculence, intransigence, demagoguery, and callous disregard for the best interests of the region," contemporaneous events reminded him of events that had taken place in the South in 1850.[10] Rather than dealing with present while preparing for the future, he felt that many in the South were content to, "look backward to an era that is dead and that is merely awaiting a decent burial."[11] Heaping scorn on the Supreme Court had become a favorite pastime in the region; the Ku Klux Klan had resurfaced and White Citizens' Councils were ubiquitous regardless of the long-term effects of such developments upon the people's respect for the rule of law. Thompson could concur with journalist Hodding Carter's characterization of White Citizens' Councils as "Uptown Ku Klux Klans," which having adopted modern publicity and organizational techniques often reflected the upper echelons of Southern society. Thompson sensed that the permissive attitude toward lawlessness and violence in the South also "[gave] every indication of getting out of hand" as had happened earlier during Reconstruction. He also perceived signs that a well-known historical pattern had resurfaced, as "Southern whites again had renewed the complaints" that had worked very well in the past, namely of "being misunderstood and maligned." Many in the region bewailed their fate and disparaged the uncharitable attitudes of Northerners, implying that if only they were left alone, they would finally get around to "[solving] the problem." To this Thompson replied, "despite 80 years of being 'let alone,' the result [is] that the region is no better off, as far as race relations are concerned, than it was in 1877," and he concluded, "It appears that the lessons of history, and much less, of common sense, have little effect upon the mentality of much of the region."[12]

This situation led Thompson to recommit the *Journal* to providing its readers with insights that history could give into the region's current turmoil via "Some Lessons of History and Common Sense," and he designed not only his spring 1956 editorial but also much of the *Journal*'s spring 1956 issue to reflect that theme. To this end, Thompson asked two colleagues at Howard University, Herbert O. Reid, professor of law, and John Hope Franklin, professor of history, to examine respectively the legality of interposition, or the assertion of states' rights to block federal initiatives, and the historical roots of the then current crisis. In addition, he asked Robert C. Weaver, an economist who was a seasoned, federal administrator and former member of the group of African American intellectuals known as the "Black Cabinet" during the administration of Franklin Roosevelt, to distill some basic lessons from the conflict over desegregation.

In his editorial, Thompson shared some of the insights that he had gleaned from reading the articles by Franklin, Weaver, and Reid. Franklin's analysis of the deplorable effects of a long history of misguided decision-making on Southern development after Reconstruction impressed Thompson, and he noted: "Professor Franklin has shown that in the past when faced by dilemmas, fancied or real, the South has consistently chosen . . . the ones most injurious to its own best interest, and the current desegregation problem is no exception."[13] Moreover, Franklin found that the control of Southern resources by Europeans and Northern outsiders had its genesis in Southern leaders' refusal "to join hands with their Negro fellows to forge a dynamic and effective new order."[14]

Another lesson that Thompson took from Weaver's "Some Basic Issues in Desegregation" was that the policy of appeasement inevitably ends in failure. "Dr. Weaver emphasizes a very important lesson of history," Thompson stated, "when he tells us that the soft-pedaling of the civil rights issues, as some well-meaning people have counseled, is the surest way to succumb to Southern racism as obtained in the 1890s."[15] On the other hand, Thompson appreciated Reid's careful and clinical analysis of the theory of interposition, which suggested that as they pledged their allegiance to this theory, Southern politicians realized that interposition would take them about as far as "a dead horse."[16] Moreover, "those who propose it [interposition] know [that the tactic will end in failure], but are merely using it as a diversionary and delaying tactic."[17] Reid further noted that their real objective was that of maintaining segregation for as long as possible.

"Speaking of diversionary tactics," Thompson continued, "the most recent move on the part of some of the white South to delay, if not frustrate implementation of the Court's decision is the issuance of a 'Manifesto,' signed by some one hundred Southern Congressmen."[18] Thompson regarded this "declaration [as] a considerably watered-down version of some of the 'Interposition' resolutions adopted by a few states, and [thought that it] was motivated by a none-too-thinly disguised combination of political expedience, historical intransigence, and considered demagoguery."[19] He found it ironic that despite "the fact that news releases had been sent out the day before [the announcement], at the very time the statement was being presented to the Senate," the Supreme Court issued a ruling in *Florida ex. Rel. Hawkins v. Board of Control of Florida* (1956) that further eroded their position.[20] In response to *Florida ex. Rel. Hawkins v. Board of Control of Florida* (1956), however, the Florida State Board of Education on March 21, 1956, revised the admissions requirements for the University of Florida to include standardized examinations.[21]

Because it was likely that the "Manifesto" would "provoke on a much larger scale more and more intemperate acts on the part of less responsible Southern whites," Thompson devoted more than 25 percent of his editorial to exploring its implications. First, he considered it as nothing less than an act of intimidation that was designed to bring desegregation to a halt, making it increasingly difficult for African Americans and Southern whites to have civil conversations or to devise solutions for moving desegregation forward.[22] The "Manifesto" could succeed only by reducing available options to absolutes such as "yes" or "no," leaving the "NAACP and many other agencies and individuals who stand for law and order and for patience in dealing with a difficult problem," few choices beyond pressing forward with litigation including that seeking monetary damages. Another purpose of the "Manifesto" was to make the NAACP seem as obstructionist as White Citizens' Councils, despite the fact that the NAACP for some time had indicated its willingness to negotiate. While it was willing to "go slow," the NAACP also insisted, and reasonably so, that school officials take some steps toward implementation. Thompson believed that the NAACP knew enough about history to understand that it could not "go fishing," or wait for the resistance movement to collapse from exhaustion.[23]

By spring 1956, Thompson visualized desegregation as a serious problem that might lead to a larger discovery. "Despite the confused picture at the present," Thompson found, "several reasons to hope for an early and constructive resolution of the issue of desegregation."[24] He gained this impression from his reading and interpretation of the surveys conducted by "practically all of the 'national' newspapers and magazines which have sent their reporters into the South" whose journalists' reportage suggested that "desegregation is inevitable, and within a reasonably short time, in some cases much shorter than even many Negroes dare hope."[25] He also based his conclusions on "softer," more qualitative data whose provenience he did not cite, and perhaps, on the coverage of the Montgomery Bus Boycott and other acts of African American agency. As he reflected, Thompson allowed himself to envision the birth of a new spirit in the South similar to that he and the other African American educators meeting at Hot Springs, Arkansas, had welcomed in October 1954.

"Some Lessons of History and Common Sense" suggested that Thompson's interpretation of developments in South had led him to two major conclusions. First, he noted that by 1956, the leadership ranks of Afro-America often comprised those who identified as New Negroes—the scholar/activists to whom historian Rayford W. Logan referred as "Disciples of Du Bois" had replaced leaders who had relied on forbearance and appealing to whites for concessions. With his characteristic candor, in this editorial Thompson spoke as a "Disciple of Du Bois" when he asserted, "we will not make the mistake we made before the turn of the century, when we were intimidated or cajoled into accepting as a fact that [segregation] was a sectional rather than a national problem." Moreover, he continued, "the white South is rapidly coming to understand that a new Negro leadership has arisen in many Southern local communities, and that unlike the 1890s this leadership is neither ignorant nor afraid." Second, Thompson pointed to the economic losses and opportunity costs related to the "School Fight" that might eventually persuade Southern business leaders to support desegregation as part of their efforts to attract new business to the region. For example, Thompson cited news reports that at least twenty corporations had decided against relocating or opening new factories in the South because of the turmoil over desegregation, and he believed that financial loses eventually would persuade Southern business leaders to intervene.

In his analysis, Thompson overlooked the fact that as masses of African American workers streamed out of the South, the opportunities for gainful employment were moving in the opposite direction: from Northern cities to Southern cities and the Southern countryside. Within a few decades, this relocation of big business southward in its never-ending search for cheap labor would negatively affect African Americans' chances of attaining the American Dream as factories in the Midwest closed transforming much of the region into a "Rust Belt" characterized by declining wages, blighted cities, and high levels of unemployment. The next chapter explores the stress that racial violence in the South placed on the New Deal coalition that disintegrated during the years of "Eisenhower prosperity" as politics in the United States swerved in a conservative direction. Nonetheless, for Thompson at this time, the

"Southern Manifesto" and other acts of outrage preoccupying Southern whites were indications that "the situation [demanded] leadership on the highest level," by which he meant leadership by the president of the United States.[26]

According to a report published in the April 2, 1956, edition of the *Washington Post and Times-Herald,* the newspaper had encouraged the White House to convene a White House Conference on desegregation "to permit, under White House auspices, an exchange of views between responsible members of both races and serve a very necessary educational purpose.'"[27] Agreeing with the proposal, Thompson also thought that the exercise of presidential leadership was the only factor that could bring the contending sides to the negotiation table. His understanding of the Southern psyche told him that a White House Conference also was necessary because, he observed "only the prestige of a White House conference will allow [the white South to save face]—and face means almost as much in the South as it does in the Orient."[28]

The 1950s marked several major milestones for Thompson, and yet the struggle had begun to register its toll on his colleagues: Charles Hamilton Houston was among the first of those whose labors had been cut short by death, and in spring 1956, he honored Walter White, who after a long illness had died of heart failure on March 31, 1955. Thompson published his tribute to White in a review of *How Far the Promised Land,* the last book in White's long career as civil rights leader, author, and journalist describing White as someone whose commitment to democracy and equal rights had never waned regardless of the barbarism, such as lynching, that he had witnessed. He regarded White, who led the NAACP from 1932 to his death, as "probably the best equipped" person in the United States to evaluate the progress African Americans had made since 1896 when segregation became compulsory. White had earned his place in history not only for his ability to attract new members or raise money; more important for Thompson was the fact that "for more than 30 years [White had been] . . . in the forefront of every major battle in behalf of unconditioned Negro equality."[29] What was particularly valuable about White's account of African American progress in the modern era was that White spoke candidly, yet encouragingly, to the living. He also invited readers in the new nations in Asia and Africa to see the United States for its potential rather than its lapses related to racism. Thompson believed that White's message would continue to inspire those committed to advancing the worldwide struggle for human rights and viewed White's concluding reflection as an invaluable source of "perspective and motivation to those [such as Thompson, who were still] on the firing line."[30]

Rarely do politicians take risks that might alienate the aroused voters in the electorate who often hold the keys to victory, and so regardless of the hopes of Thompson and the editors of the *Washington Post and Times-Herald,* it was not surprising that Eisenhower refused to wager his 1956 presidential reelection bid on a White House Conference on desegregation. Eisenhower had a knack for seeming to say the right thing in his relationships with African Americans without making any concrete promises that might come back to haunt him: he was alert, self-conscious, and only willing to go far enough to convey the impression that he was being fair. After the cherry blossoms were a memory and springtime in Washington, DC, had passed, a few short months remained before the August 1956 national conventions of the Democratic Party and the Republican Party. The Democratic Party would hold its National Convention first, from August 13 to 17, 1956, in Chicago, Illinois, at the International Amphitheatre located on the south side of the city, and the Republican Party National Convention would follow immediately, from August 20 to 23, 1956, in San Francisco's Cow Palace. Many Democrats feared that Republican political strategists might "spin" desegregation into an issue that might rip the once-solidly Democratic Party South from its moorings and cost Adlai Stevenson the presidency.

Spring 1956 also was a notable time in the world of scholarly publishing. At about the time when the spring 1956 issue of the *Journal* appeared on library bookshelves, the March 1956 issue of *The Annals of the American Academy of Political and Social Science, Racial Desegregation and Integration,* edited by sociologist Ira deA. Reid, did so too. John Hope Franklin and Robert C. Weaver had published articles in the March 1956 issue of *The Annals* as well as in the spring 1956 issue of the *Journal*. The correspondence and connectivity did not end here: eight of twenty-one, or 38 percent, of the authors published in the March 1956 issue of *The Annals* had also contributed articles to previous issues of the *Journal*. They included Ambrose Caliver, David A. Lane, Jr., Rayford W. Logan, James M. Nabrit, Jr., Irene G. Osborne, and Ira deA. Reid, the issue's editor.

A year before his promotion to professor of education at Howard University, Thompson had published "The Educational Achievements of Negro Children" in *The American Negro*, the November 1928 issue of *The Annals*. Later, Thompson had modeled the *Journal* after scholarly magazines that he respected, such as the *School Review* and *Elementary School Journal* founded by Charles H. Judd, his mentor at Chicago, and *The Annals of the American Academy of Political and Social Science*. Indeed, in biographical statements several times in the 1950s and 1960s Thompson noted his membership in the American Academy of Political and Social Science.[31] Consistent with the assessment that Thompson offered in winter 1956 in "The Twenty-Fifth Volume of the *Journal of Negro Education*," the *Journal* had made great strides since its inception; it had cultivated a coherent literature related to African American education that also had a demonstrable effect on public policy, especially the policy of segregation. Along the way, Thompson had cultivated several generations of scholars, including some who met or exceeded the standards of *The Annals*, one of the oldest and most prestigious scholarly journals in the United States. In a sense, *The Annals* and the *Journal* pursued complementary research agendas that emphasized "the free exchange of ideas." *The Annals* was much more expansive in scope, and yet the *Journal* mirrored that breadth in the specialization of African American education with some attention to the arts and culture. Their March 1956 and spring 1956 issues respectively gave the impression of being "in conversation," or being part of a discourse community, although the magazines were designed and published independently. Several contributors to the 1956 issue of the Yearbook appeared to have agreed with such an assessment: several of the contributors cited work published in the March 1956 issue of *The Annals*, especially Harold C. Fleming's thoughtful essay, "Resistance Movements and Racial Desegregation."[32]

As the second anniversary of *Brown I* (1954) approached, racial animosities in the South appeared to be on the increase rather than dissipating. In that climate, Thompson thought it important to measure exactly how much desegregation in public education had taken place, where, and with what success. Therefore, he designed a follow-up to the 1955 issue of the Yearbook, *The Desegregation Decision—One Year Afterward*.[33] Now that a full year had passed, it would be possible to capture the full measure of the progress made, or as he said, the "lack of progress" made toward implementation of the US Supreme Court's decision in the *School Segregation Cases*. To enhance the value of the 1955 and 1956 issues of the Yearbook for purposes of comparison, Thompson persuaded "the same contributors who participated in the 1955 Yearbook, with one or two exceptions" to contribute an updated assessment for the 1956 Yearbook. Thompson informed readers that, "due to circumstances beyond our control specific appraisal of the status in Georgia is not included. It should be noted, however," he continued, "that the situation in this state [Georgia] in not unlike that in other states such as Mississippi and Virginia where there has developed a technique of defiance and resistance."[34]

As early as 1954, the response of Virginians to desegregation had been baffling for African Americans born in the South such as Thompson who thought he knew the state and its people. Having spent his high school and college years in Richmond studying at Virginia Union University, Thompson could not have been more wrong: Virginia, despite its location in the Upper South and its reputation for milder race relations than the norm, had become as receptive to resistance and defiance as Mississippi. The strong public support for resistance that showed no signs of abating in summer 1956 also astonished Thompson. The South seemed to have split in half with some states, mainly the Border States, respecting the *Brown* decision and upholding the rule of law, and the other half on the verge of disorder and chaos. Thompson ended the shortest editorial of his career by noting that: "What is most striking, however, is the fact that those states which expressed defiance of the decision in 1955 have continued to do so and set up more specific means of implementing their defiance." He ended with his customary note of encouragement to those on "the firing line." "While the picture is not as encouraging as it appeared in 1955 . . . considerable progress has taken place; sufficient to suggest that the problem will be solved earlier than many people suspect."[35]

The 1956 issue of the Yearbook differed from the 1955 Yearbook in other respects that Thompson did not mention in his editorial. Whereas Carter, Marshall, Parrish, and Valien had provided critical summaries in 1955, only Valien prepared a critical summary for the 1956 issue of the Yearbook. In agreement with Thompson's appraisal, Valien's article also saw the South as comprised of two worlds held together by an accident of geography. He began by pointing to the growth of resistance movements in the region and noted that "the period has been marked by a growth in organized opposition to the Supreme Court's decision which, in the Deep South, approaches anarchy in some instances and overt subversion of the national government in others."[36] Meanwhile, the supporters of desegregation scored their main victories in courtrooms, rather than in schools or classrooms. At year's end, Valien found there was more "significant progress in desegregation . . . outside of education" than inside it, that Southern white moderates and Southern politicians were most at fault for allowing the division of Southern society into warring camps, and that Southern white moderates lacked meaningful influence in their local communities.[37] Valien reserved his strongest criticism for Southern politicians for their lack of "political integrity and legal ethics" and for spearheading the resistance movement noting that several:

> of the Southern attorneys and political leaders in Arkansas, Florida, and other states who [had gained notoriety for] influencing the U. S. Supreme Court to grant their states [additional] time for adjustment in [*Brown II*] are now among the leaders of the resistance movements in their states.[38]

Valien also cited Harold C. Fleming's essay in the March 1956 issue of *The Annals* that had found that the resistance to desegregation was highest in those places where White Citizens' Councils and similar resistance groups exercised control of politics. Valien and Fleming were both native Southerners, and Valien asserted,

> Fleming . . . points out that in at least four Southern states political control is in the hands of politicians who are wholly sympathetic to the aims and methods of the resistance groups, while in four additional states the resistance groups exert strong political influence on the legislature and upon political officeholders.[39]

The political influence of the resistance movements was strongest in those rural "Black Belt" counties distinguished by large numbers of African American residents as well as by the near total absence of African Americans from voting. Whereas Valien captured the extensive use of intimidation and coercion by resistance groups and their wholesale attack on civil rights, he omitted Fleming's stronger point about the interest of some leaders of resistance groups in using them to launch a much broader political movement. By reading an Associated Press interview of W. J. Simmons, executive secretary of the Jackson, Mississippi, [White Citizens'] Council published in the August 22, 1955, edition of the Montgomery (Alabama) *Advertiser*, Fleming had discovered the much grander ambitions of some of its leaders for developing White Citizens' Councils into the base for a formidable political organization. Fleming quoted Simmons as suggesting that:

> [the White Citizens' Council] is much more than a white supremacist group and I think it is much more than a protectionist group. I think it is fundamentally the first real stirrings of a conservative revolt in this country, judging by the responses we've gotten from other states. . . . Some of the people who are attracted to this movement may not be concerned about the Negro. What would be classed as the old white supremacist movement has no place. It is too narrow.[40]

Much as Fleming had done, Valien felt that the use of economic reprisals by White Citizens' Councils was likely to backfire, especially in places where many African Americans resided. They also agreed that the most signficant development in the South in the mid-1950s was "the growing consciousness and utilization of the Negro of his economic power. The bus boycotts in Montgomery and Tallahassee and the economic boycotts in Orangeburg and other places have demonstrated a remarkable effectiveness and unity of purpose."[41]

Educational Desegregation, 1956, was the last Yearbook of Thompson's editorship that examined desegregation at the elementary and secondary levels of education in "the 17 segregated school states and District of Columbia." After summer 1956, Thompson resumed the research cycle that he had begun years earlier, having adapted it from Du Bois' *Atlanta University Studies*. Following Du Bois' example, Thompson would usually wait from seven to ten years before reexamining a problem explored in an earlier Yearbook, but would make exceptions when it appeared that a policy window might open and it might to possible to win the support of legislators and policymakers for his preferred solutions. For him, desegregation represented an interim policy goal; it was not synonymous with the wholesome interaction of human beings based on equality that was his real objective. Meanwhile, like Walter White, Thompson's major task was that of creating a sound roadmap for other researchers to either follow or improve upon by blazing new trails and extending knowledge in new directions. His resumption of the *Journal*'s research agenda and its previous cycle of research rested upon his optimism as well as his realization that the wheels of progress often turned painfully slowly. His emphasis on critical appraisal and systematic measurements in his search for tipping points would give in-depth treatment to issues such as *The Negro Voter in the South* (1957) or *African Education South of the Sahara* (1961). In spring and summer of 1956, however, Thompson acted more as a cartographer—he mapped the strongholds of segregation, the places were desegregation had stalled after it had made some inroads, and distinguished the former from the places where people of goodwill had resolved to give the process of desegregation a fighting chance.

NOTES

1. John H. McCray, "Thugs Fail to frighten Civic Leader," Afro American (Washington, DC), December 6, 1955, 1–2, accessed July 2, 2017, https://news.google.com/newspapers/p/afro?nid=BeIT3YV5QzEC&dat=19551206&printsec=frontpage&hl=en.
2. Charles H. Thompson, "Editorial Comment: The Twenty-Fifth Volume of the *Journal of Negro Education*," *The Journal of Negro Education*, 25 no. 1 (Winter 1956): 1; Charles H. Thompson, "Editorial Comment: Why a *Journal of Negro Education*?" *The Journal of Negro Education*, 1, no. 1 (April 1932): 1.
3. Thompson, "The Twenty-Fifth Volume of the *Journal of Negro Education*," 1.
4. Ibid.
5. Ibid., 2.
6. William Attwood, "The Position of Jews in America Today," *Look*, 19: 27–35, November 29, 1955; as cited in Thompson, "The Twenty-Fifth Volume of the *Journal of Negro Education*," 3.
7. Ibid.
8. Ibid.
9. Ibid.
10. Charles H. Thompson, "Editorial Comment: Some Lessons of History and Common Sense," *The Journal of Negro Education*, 25, no. 2 (Spring 1956): 91.
11. Ibid., 91.
12. Ibid.
13. Ibid.
14. John Hope Franklin, "Desegregation—The South's Newest Dilemma," *The Journal of Negro Education*, 25, no. 2 (Spring 1956): 95.
15. Thompson, "Some Lessons of History and Common Sense," 91.
16. Ibid.
17. Ibid.
18. Ibid.; Justin Driver, "Op-Ed: 60 Years Later the Southern Manifesto is as Alive as Ever," *Los Angeles Times*, accessed September 21, 2017, http://www.latimes.com/opinion/op-ed/la-oe-0311-driver-southern-manifesto-anniversary-20160311-story.html. The Southern Manifesto succeeded in undercutting the support for desegregation in the North and limiting the reach of the *Brown* decision, according to Driver.
19. Thompson, "Some Lessons of History and Common Sense," 92.
20. Ibid.
21. The State Board of Control–Florida, "The Problem of Entrance Requirements for the State Universities in Florida," *The Journal of Negro Education*, 25, no. 2 (Spring 1956): 200–1. In this issue, Thompson also published the remarkable "Resolution of the Faculty and Staff of the South Carolina State College," in support of the NAACP and desegregation even if their support prompted state officials to close South Carolina State College. See "Resolution of the Faculty and Staff of the South Carolina State College," *The Journal of Negro Education*, 25, no. 2 (Spring 1956): 197–99.
22. Thompson, "Some Lessons of History and Common Sense," 92.
23. Ibid.
24. Ibid., 93.

25. Ibid.
26. Ibid., 93–94.
27. Ibid., 94.
28. Ibid.
29. Charles H. Thompson, "Review of: *How Far the Promised Land by Walter White*," *The Journal of Negro Education*, 25, no. 2 (Spring 1956): 142.
30. Ibid., 142–43.
31. Charles H. Thompson, questionnaire completed and returned to Mr. Robert C. Cook, editor, Trustees, Presidents and Deans of American Colleges and Universities, Who's Who in American Education, Inc., 110 Seventh Avenue, North, Nashville 1, Tennessee, December 26, 1957; "Danforth Foundation Questionnaire," June 5, 1961; Questionnaire for Leaders in American Science, circa June 30, 1963, School of Education Papers, Moorland-Spingarn Research Center, Howard University Archives, Howard University, Box 1894, *Journal of Negro Education*.
32. "Since 1889, *The American Academy of Political and Social Science* has served as a forum for the free exchange of ideas among the well informed and intellectually curious. In this era of specialization, few scholarly periodicals cover the scope of societies and politics like *The Annals*. Each volume is guest edited by outstanding scholars and experts in the topics studied and presents more than 200 pages of timely, in-depth research on a significant topic of concern." "About this Journal: The ANNALS of the American Academy of Political and Social Science," Sage Journals, accessed July 25, 2017, http://journals.sagepub.com/home/ann.
33. Charles H. Thompson, "Educational Desegregation—1956," *The Journal of Negro Education*, 25, no. 3 (Summer 1956): 203.
34. Ibid.
35. Ibid.
36. Preston Valien, "The Status of Educational Desegregation, 1956: A Critical Summary," *The Journal of Negro Education*, 25, no. 3 (Summer 1956): 359.
37. Ibid.
38. Ibid., 361.
39. Ibid.
40. Bem Price, Montgomery (Alabama) *Advertiser*, August 22, 1955, as quoted in Harold C. Fleming, "Resistance Movements and Racial Desegregation," *The Annals of the American Academy of Political and Social Science* 304, *Racial Desegregation and Integration* (March 1956): 50.
41. Preston Valien, "The Status of Educational Desegregation, 1956: A Critical Summary," 368.

FIVE

The Implosion of the New Deal Coalition

Two qualities that distinguished Thompson's fall 1956 editorial, "The Dilemma of Negro Voters," which was timed to appear within days of Election Day, November 6, 1956, and recorded his thinking on the eve of the election, were its thoughtfulness, which is what his readers expected of him, and his evenhandedness that removed any signs of partisanship from the discussion. In Thompson's steady hands, a topic such as voting in a national election afforded the opportunity to probe features of the American character, and he identified a tendency to use half-measures and marry this to expediency when shaping human expectations.

Thompson brought to the discussion not only his belief that it was essential for scholars to be activists but also his habit of viewing problems carefully and with the patience of a seasoned researcher. Offering his comments in the politically charged atmosphere of Washington, DC, Thompson was aware that critics in Congress often pounced on academics associated with Howard University, branding them as visionary or, worse, as unpatriotic. Although he was a professor, as an African American teacher Thompson was not safe from acts of retaliation such as those endured by his colleagues in the South. Moreover, he knew that the acceptability of his editorial voice depended upon the support of Mordecai Wyatt Johnson, the president of Howard University, who his faults notwithstanding, was noted for advocating and endorsing academic freedom.

As a resident of the District of Columbia in 1956, Thompson lacked political representation in Congress, a dilemma that many African American voters in the South had faced for over sixty years. If understanding a problem requires that one also understand its context, then it is equally true that no social movement operates in isolation. In his brief, two-page reflection, Thompson offered his readers his perspective on the implications of politics for civil rights, based on a survey conducted before the 1956 presidential election that also served as an overture for policy research in support of the National Association for the Advancement of Colored People's (NAACP's) campaign for voting rights. According to Thompson's editorial, limited choices and the winner-take-all US electoral process created "a difficult problem" for many voters in the United States.[1] If they refused to cast a protest vote, then voters had few, viable options beyond choosing among the candidates nominated by the Republican or Democratic Party. In other words, like buying manufactured clothes "off the rack," they had to decide between Republican or Democratic candidates, messaging, imagery, and worldview.

In addition, race and race relations complicated the situation greatly for African Americans, given the economic, social, and psychological dimensions of their lives. Initially, neither party protected them from the indignities of Jim Crow, but because of "an undue sense of gratitude to the party of Lincoln for abolishing slavery," African Americans in the North "voted overwhelmingly for Republican nominees in both state and national elections," a trend that continued broken until 1912.[2] It was only after "the second administration of Franklin D. Roosevelt" that African American voting behavior changed significantly, with large numbers of African Americans casting their lot with the Democratic Party.[3] That option was available to African Americans outside the South because most African Americans in the South lost the right to vote after Reconstruction: the few who managed to register to vote could not vote in the Democratic Party primary elections that held the key to winning office in the one-party South.

In this editorial, Thompson next assayed the differences in the party philosophies of the Republicans and Democrats that compounded the difficulties that African American voters had to negotiate. According to Thompson, "The philosophy of the Republican Party seems to have been and still appears to be, that what is good for 'big business' is best for the country, in that the benefits will trickle down to the masses; and if the benefits do not reach all of the masses, it is their [the masses'] fault."[4] On the other hand, the philosophy of the Democratic Party seemed closer to African Americans' interests: "['in *theory*,'] . . . The primary concern of government is for the welfare of all of the people, and particularly [that] of the 'common' [person] since the prosperity of the nation is only validly measured by the extent to which he [or she] prospers."[5]

Nonetheless, Thompson felt that the stated differences were more imaginary than real, and in 1956, with the leaders of the Democratic Party concerned about holding Southern whites within the party to have any chance of winning the presidential election, at the Democratic National Convention they permitted the adoption of "a [civil rights] plank . . . [that gave] very little encouragement to Negroes."[6] Thompson also thought that the Republican Party had shortchanged African American voters, its most galling failing being the chief executive's refusal to take a firm stand in support of desegregation. Thompson found President Eisenhower's tolerant attitude toward Southern leaders' acts of defiance and resistance to the *Brown* decision exasperating. In essence, he felt that the Republican Party platform "was only a shade, if any, more encouraging. What is more, the Republican nominee has been so remiss as President in providing effective leadership in this area during the past three and a half years, and particularly since the Supreme Court's May 17, 1954 decision, that it appears extremely doubtful that Negroes would be any better off if the Republican nominees were elected."[7] Thompson closed his fall 1956 editorial ready to collect and weigh the evidence that the election results would provide to detect "what course Negro voters would pursue."[8] In this essay, Thompson captured a dynamic moment in US politics before the New Deal coalition collapsed and the South moved from the Democratic column and tilted toward the Republicans.

When the *Journal*'s winter 1957 issue went to press, the tabulation of the 1956 election data was complete: Eisenhower had won unprecedented support of among African American voters in a landslide reelection victory that garnered him and his vice-presidential candidate, Richard M. Nixon, 457 Electoral College votes.[9] In accounting for Eisenhower's success in attracting African American and, more significantly, Southern white voters in 1956, Henry Lee Moon, the NAACP public relations director, offered the following explanation:

> Negro voters in 1956, like other citizens, were concerned about peace and prosperity, taxes and the atom bomb. School desegregation and other civil rights were also vital issues with them as they were with white Southerners. . . . Ironically, the civil rights issue was a factor which, in many localities in the South, united opposing groups behind the same candidate [namely, Dwight D. Eisenhower].[10]

The growing split in the body politic concerned Thompson, and in his winter 1957 editorial, "Desegregation 1956; Prospects 1957," he weighed the losses and gains of the effort to create a culture of respect that many Southern whites resisted and considered heretical. With an accountant's precision, he placed the "wins" and "losses" of the previous year (1956) in perspective in order to determine the net outcome. Such periodic assessments buoyed Thompson's optimism and helped him deal with the fatigue of assigning too much value to transitory issues. Thompson added his voice to that of Preston Valien and others who detected "what seems now to be a fairly well defined pattern" in the resistance of desegregation in bus transportation, for example. Initially, there was no violence, followed by "premeditated acts of violence against Negroes and any whites who might sympathize with them."[11] Beyond showing that desegregation would not work, the goal was to "intimidate Negro leaders" into submission.[12]

Thompson pointed to recent polling that suggested the "'desegregation sentiment' [was] growing in the country as a whole."[13] Despite nearly two years of anarchy and "many reactionary efforts to maintain the status quo," what the polls surprisingly showed was that more Americans supported desegregation in 1956 than had done so in 1954, rising from 54 to 63 percent. Because the Supreme Court had not wavered from the principle it had set in *Brown* (1954), the federal courts also adhered to that precedent with few exceptions. Thompson found the Court's consistency especially encouraging because he believed that it "has naturally strengthened not only the legal position of those pressing for desegregation, but even more important, their moral position."[14] He applauded the stoic attitude of those African Americans in the South whom were confronted with violence and was especially pleased to note that "Negroes, to date, have refused to become terrorized."[15]

Thompson again pointed to the growth of "a grassroots Negro leadership in the South which has proved to be both sagacious and courageous" as the movement's best outcome and hope for success.[16] Because the African American church was not only a refuge but also the organizational hub for African Americans in the South, the new leaders' connection to it gave them added protection and support. According to Thompson, the rise of these new leaders and the widespread support that they enjoyed was unequivocal proof that African Americans in the South were dissatisfied with Jim Crow and had reached that conclusion independently and voluntarily. "The spectacle of Negro ministers going to jail in the interest of their cause has shaken Southern white complacency more than would be acknowledged," he noted.[17]

The rise of principled African American leaders in the South affirmed Thompson's belief in quality higher education as an instrument for developing sound leadership. Many of the young African American ministers such as Martin Luther King, Jr., had completed baccalaureate and graduate studies or divinity schools, their training having prepared them to address their communities' needs while persuading people from all walks of life to join them in their campaigns for justice. The winter 1957 issue of the *Journal* also is significant because of Thompson's short editorial note saying farewell to Charles Spurgeon Johnson and acknowledging Johnson's contributions to sociology and the study of race relations.

Johnson, president of Fisk University, died on October 27, 1956, exactly two years after the adjournment of the Hot Springs conference. In their youth, Johnson and Thompson had attended Virginia Union University where they received mentoring from Joshua Baker Simpson, Union's renowned professor of Greek, Latin, and the social sciences. In the dedication page of *The Negro College Graduate* (1933), Johnson had acknowledged Joshua Baker Simpson and Robert E. Park's contributions to his development as a teacher, scholar, and human being when he recognized them as "two great teachers." As had Thompson in 1925, Johnson also completed his doctorate at Chicago around 1920. Johnson had nearly died from the stab wounds that he received during the Chicago race riot during the bloody summer of 1919, and so he had firsthand knowledge of the terror that racism and racial hatred could unleash. In a note to Johnson's last article, "A Southern Negro's View of the South," originally published in "the *New York Times Magazine* section on Sunday, September 23, 1956," Thompson assessed Johnson's final work as: "undoubtedly one of the best, if not the best, statements on the present South and the race problem that has appeared in print."[18] With the permission of the *New York Times* and Johnson's estate, Thompson reprinted the article in the *Journal*'s winter 1957 issue "both because of its intrinsic value, and as a tribute to the untiring efforts which the author had put forth in the field of race relations for upwards of 40 years."[19]

Johnson began his essay by noting that when people spoke about the "Southern point of view and way of life," they invariably omitted the region's African Americans' "viewpoint." Doing so was simply "part of the Southern way of life."[20] A case in point, noted Johnson, was the October 1954 conference of African American educators held in Hot Springs, Arkansas, whose position paper issued at the conclusion of the conference was "one of the most ignored public invitations on record," and he quoted liberally from it.[21] Johnson believed that the South was "separatist" in spirit, and that while African Americans in the region focused on cultivating a national rather than regional identity, this was not because African Americans regarded themselves as inferiors despite "[earning lower wages or [having] fewer years of school." Instead, he claimed, "there has been a measurable loss of Negro respect for white pretenders to a superiority that can only be sustained by legal statutes and illegal violence, or the threat of it."[22] Johnson did not think that a "conversion" among the people he referred to as "grass roots" (the Southern white working class) would lead to significant improvements in African Americans' "civil rights status." On the contrary, he felt it wise of African Americans in the region to think that only the federal government could author improvements in their well-being in terms of "employment and wages, voting, personal security, access to cultural facilities, and other requisites of democratic living."[23] Regarding segregation, Johnson cautioned against believing that "the tired policy of moderation" would work, and he doubted whether there was any genius in taking "a tortuous logic that would use the tragic results of inequality to establish the need of continuing it."[24]

In Johnson's opinion, the real issue involved in the school segregation cases was not educational, sociological, or cultural; the real issue was one of morals, ethics, and justice. He thought that it was foolhardy to think that one could allow someone to deprive a neighbor of freedom without someday facing the same predicament oneself. Similarly, Johnson believed that the South would regret the day it accepted lawlessness as a substitute for discussion and compromise. Disrespecting the Supreme Court was especially dangerous in his view because "Where there is repudiation of the integrity of the Court, our ultimate constitutional authority, on one issue, there is repudiation of the integrity of the Court and the law on any and all issues."[25]

It was their faith in democracy that had allowed African Americans to put up with the indignities of Jim Crow, Johnson believed, and thus the crisis over desegregation masked a much larger moral crisis. The essay also echoed the need to make democracy more than a hollow promise to the new nations in Asia and Africa as the United States became a superpower, Johnson's comments resonating with the ideas endorsed in the Hot Springs position paper. Johnson concluded by expressing his faith in democracy: "The essence of our system of government and life is voluntary cooperation in a democratic process that respects the dignity and rights of individuals. Our faith in the power of the human spirit to achieve the ends of a free society has given hope to millions of [humans] over the world. We cannot default on this promise. This is our moral challenge in a national crisis."[26]

A few months later, in the *Journal*'s spring 1957 issue, Thompson had cause to mourn the loss of yet another colleague, psychologist Howard Hale Long. Since the 1930s, Long and Thompson had worked in support of a policy research agenda aimed at extending human rights to many of the world's people, and Long had produced in 1935 a paper, "Some Psychogenic Hazards of Segregated Education for Negroes," for the *Journal*'s Yearbook. In a note to Long's paper "The Relative Learning Capacities of Negroes and Whites," Thompson had written: "This paper was completed only a few days before Dr. Long's death. It is published posthumously, not only because of its value *per se*, but as a tribute to one of the early psychologists who pointed out the invalidity of some of the studies based on the old army tests employed during World War I."[27] In his article, Long strongly restated his opposition to those skeptics who disputed the effects of environmental factors such as educational opportunities, income, and wealth on African Americans' level of achievement.

In his spring 1957 editorial, Thompson also welcomed Ghana's emergence as the first West African colony to gain independence "in our time." Although he considered "The Gold Coast Revolution" notable, he admitted that it had caught him "and undoubtedly others" by surprise because he had dismissed reports that Ghana would become "an independent state . . . within the British Commonwealth" as "propaganda" produced by the "Colonial Ministry."[28] Thompson informed his readers that Ghana became an independent state on March 6, 1957, and was "renamed after the celebrated West African empire which flourished in part of this region [of Africa] from the 4th to the 13th centuries." He also noted that in addition to "official representatives from some 51 nations and thousands of foreign visitors," Vice President Richard Nixon led the "official delegation from the United States" and that approximately eleven African Americans "attended the ceremonies as private citizens."[29]

Thompson had composed his editorial in early March 1957 using data from a book that "luckily . . . came to [his] desk, the autobiography of the young Prime Minister of the new Ghana," *Ghana—The Autobiography of Kwame Nkrumah* (1957) published by Thomas Nelson and Sons, as well as Bankole Timothy's 198-page biography, *Kwame Nkrumah*. In a "capsule review" in the October 1956 issue of *Foreign Affairs* historian Henry L. Roberts had described Timothy's book as a celebratory and yet critical account of Nkrumah's life and rise to leadership. Armed with such data, Thompson probed for the significance of the end of nearly 120 years of colonial rule when Ghana distinguished itself as the second sub-Saharan nation to gain its independence. In as much as Thompson believed in the concept of self-government, and independence for India had been a consistent theme of his editorial content during World War II, as early as 1934, he had expressed his opposition to imperialism and colonialism the world over. However, before March 6, 1957, he felt that independence would occur in sub-Saharan Africa "sometime in the distant future."[30] Thompson thought it fair to rank Nkrumah alongside Gandhi and Nehru, noting that like these leaders Nkrumah had been so committed to Ghanaian independence that he and other leaders had accepted imprisonment while rejecting calls for violence or armed resistance.[31] Symbolically, Nkrumah personified the policy of "positive action," and this approach to politics had attracted a mass following when he ceased to be an expatriate and returned to Ghana.[32] According to Thompson, the motto that motivated members of Nkrumah's Convention People's Party (CPP) was "To fight relentlessly by all constitutional means for the achievement of 'self-government NOW.'"[33]

He pointed out that it was through the application of "positive action" that Ghanaians had successfully disrupted and "tied up the entire industrial and political life of the Colony," which was the world's largest cocoa producer. Initially, the colonial government had attempted to break the movement by arresting and imprisoning its leaders, yet mounting pressure from world opinion and ongoing civil disobedience campaigns eventually resulted in Nkrumah's election while in prison to "a seat in the provisional Assembly in an election in which the CPP was victorious by a stunning majority." For Thompson, Ghanaian independence "has undoubtedly raised the hopes and redoubled the efforts of colonial peoples in other parts of Africa and the world, who are striving for independence. It is our hope that they will be equally successful; and in as short a time."[34]

Ghana was free and independent, but the same was not true for nearly 90 percent of the African Americans in the Southern United States, regardless of their stances on desegregation. Significant barriers prevented all but a handful of African Americans in the South from exercising their right to vote, and as the resistance to public school desegregation strengthened, the movement to remove African Americans in the South from the voting rolls gained momentum. Thompson appreciated the reasoning of those critics of litigation who felt that it was a poor substitute for the right to vote, and he found merit in the position of the "many competent observers" who suggested that a substantial increase in African Americans' voting strength could break the impasse over desegregation.[35]

Because most African Americans in the South did not vote in 1957, legislators holding racist views often represented their communities while touting the benefits of free and fair elections outside the United States. Moreover, Thompson thought that African Americans in the South in 1957 were in more political jeopardy than their ancestors were when the Three-Fifths Compromise of 1787 was binding. During the 1950s, the NAACP, the Reverend Dr. Martin Luther King, Jr., and prominent labor leaders had endorsed voting rights campaigns designed to extend and strengthen the New Deal coalition. Consequently, Thompson designed the *Journal*'s 1957 Yearbook, *The Negro Voter in the South*, to focus the attention of leading scholars and practitioners on reducing voting discrimination in that region. Although it was necessary to catalog the various hindrances to voting, Thompson felt that the Yearbook's real value would be in providing sound data and practical solutions for reaching the goal of adding three million African American voters in the South that the NAACP and the Southern Christian Leadership Conference had set.

The 1957 Yearbook featured an essay-based symposium in which Florence B. Irving, a research assistant at the Southern Regional Council; law professor James M. Nabrit, Jr.; and political scientist Daniel S. Strong offered their differing visions of "The Future of the Negro Voter in the South." Political analyst Samuel Lubell and Roy Wilkins, executive secretary or head of the NAACP, then assessed "The Future of the Negro Voter in the United States." Many of the Yearbook's chapters were in development when the Civil Rights Bill of 1957 "[had] passed the House of Representatives and [was] . . . under debate in the Senate."[36] In the Yearbook, historians C. Vann Woodward and John Hope Franklin also traced the extension and denial of African American voting rights in the South, and the NAACP's Thurgood Marshall chronicled "The Rise and Collapse of 'The White Democratic Primary'" with a focus on the efforts of African Americans in Texas to end that practice. In "Some Legislative Consequences of Negro Disfranchisement," Robert C. Weaver and Hortense W. Gabel, then administrators with the Temporary State Housing Rent Commission in New York State, related the denial of voting rights to African Americans in the rural South to the defeat of progressive legislation on the national scene. Weaver and Gabel demonstrated that Southerners in Congress often held the balance of power, with enough votes to kill legislation mandating fair employment practices, extending workers' rights, or reducing immigration restrictions. Working in coalition with conservative Republicans, Southern Democrats reduced the federal appropriations for public housing by 97 percent in 1957. They voted to kill bills to extend subsidies to middle-class homeowners as well as the natural gas industry. Accordingly, Weaver and Gabel concluded that significant increases in voting by African Americans in the South, especially those in the rural "Black Belt" counties, needed to occur for any really progressive legislation to become law.

Irving's contribution to the symposium was her familiarity with the statistical data on Southern voting, and she showed that beginning from a baseline of 140,000 African American voters in 1940 that "at least 1,238,038 Negroes were registered in the eleven Southern states" in 1956. The NAACP's voter registration clinics in North Carolina, for example, accounted for a 16 percent increase from 125,000 to 145,000 voters. On the other hand, as African American voters were added to the rolls in some counties in North Carolina, others were purged from those in "Louisiana, Mississippi, Alabama, Georgia, and [ironically,] North Carolina," negating any gains from NAACP voter registration efforts.[37] In June 1957, the Southern Christian Leadership Conference, led by the Reverend Dr. Martin Luther King, Jr., announced plans, in partnership with Vice President Richard M. Nixon, to register three million African American voters in the Southern states by 1958. Based on Irving's report that there were 4,980,743 Southern nonwhites of voting age in the region, the Southern Christian Leadership Conference planned to register 60.2 percent of the pool of potential voters in order to double the number of registered African American voters in the South. This plan set off alarms in many quarters of the region, prompting new efforts at curtailing African American voting and adding to the realignment of politics in the South.[38]

Nearly nine million or 52.5 percent of Southern whites had registered to vote in 1956 compared with 24.9 percent of African Americans of voting age. Irving attributed this gap in voter registration to economic reprisals such as those orchestrated by White Citizens' Councils as well as to gerrymandering and redistricting schemes such as that designed specifically to disfranchise faculty at the Tuskegee Institute, and illustrating the open disregard for qualifications when disqualifying eligible African American voters. In a similar vein, examining the chicanery involved in using literacy tests to qualify uneducated Southern whites to vote while routinely disqualifying college educated African Americans by asking them to correctly answer ridiculous questions such as "How many bubbles are there in a cake of soap?" or "How many rooms are in the courthouse?" Irving also reported that "3,420 Negro registrants in Ouachita Parish, Louisiana [were challenged], and that [White Citizens' Councils] were responsible for the contesting of some of the 5,312 Negro citizens . . . in nine other parishes" in Louisiana.[39]

When competent observers such as Attorney General Herbert Brownell, Jr., admitted that few legal protections of voting rights existed in 1957, Irving allowed that the Civil Rights Act of 1957, which Brownell supported, was a step in the right direction, considering that it "[contained] a significant provision through which voting abuses can be checked."[40] Irving ended her essay with the prediction that although the goal of registering three million African Americans voters was very ambitious, significant increases in African American voting were likely and would have positive implications for the struggle for equality in the South.[41]

Donald S. Strong believed that increases in voting were likely to occur in major cities in the South where there were fewer barriers to African American voting and where Southern whites accepted this development, however grudgingly. Strong predicted that because household incomes among African Americans in rural areas were dismally low, and few households boasted anyone completing more than five years of school, there would be few gains in African American voting in rural areas. He further related increases in African American voting to the availability of well-trained, middle-class African American leaders and because the miserable conditions in rural communities were repulsive to "an educated Negro middle class," he did not foresee major increases in African American voters in the rural communities where many low-income African Americans lived.[42]

Desegregation also had a significant effect on the behavior and voting patterns of Southern whites in that it made those in rural counties sensitive to any threat to their longstanding control, rendering African American voting an unacceptable type of militancy that justified economic reprisals, bombings, or murder. Strong also predicted that mechanization and the shift from planting cotton to raising beef cattle would sustain the exodus of African Americans from the rural areas to the cities.[43] Nonetheless, Strong felt that any further increases in African American voters would be slow because many of those who were unregistered were less motivated to do the work or hazard the risks involved in casting a ballot.[44]

James M. Nabrit, Jr., brought to the symposium the perspective of a voting rights activist who had worked in the Deep South as well as that of a lawyer who had argued before the Supreme Court. Nabrit believed that in 1957 a misunderstanding of the political process prevented African Americans from successfully "wedding" their economic interests with their concerns for civil rights. When they refused to separate the two, Nabrit predicted that politicians would not secure many African American votes without making the appropriate economic and civil rights concessions. He accordingly concluded that when African

Americans could consistently muster such discipline, then they would obtain their share of the "jobs, patronage [and] benefits of various kinds" that were the sweet fruit of the election process.[45] Whereas Strong's article focused on the effects of school desegregation and mechanization on voting in the South, Nabrit pointed out that:

> The key figure in Southern political operation is the sheriff. He is the controlling county officer; he exercises influence in many ways—in jury selection, registration, voting, in tax assessment and collection, and in law enforcement and illegal activities. His goodwill is an enormous asset. He and his deputies know the county, its citizens, and what is going on. His influence extends into municipal affairs, state politics and campaigns for Congress. The Negro's fear and mistrust of police and law enforcement officers operate as a deterrent to his challenging the sheriff's indication that [the sheriff] is opposed to registration and voting by Negroes.[46]

Thus, both Strong and Nabrit pointed to the urban North and South as offering the best opportunities for adding African American voters to the rolls in 1957. Nabrit thought that adding enough African American voters also would serve to lower the resistance to African American voting in the South, particularly if the leaders of the national political parties saw to it that county sheriffs did not interfere in the election process.[47]

In his article, Roy Wilkins also dealt with the barriers to voting at the county precinct level, attempting to quell doubts about the NAACP's voting rights strategy and the organization's overall effectiveness. In what amounted to a call to arms, he urged readers in the North to turn precinct meetings, state party councils, and "every conference with the state's national committeemen and committeewomen" into referendums on African Americans' right to vote and for those in the South to overcome the impediments to their voting.[48] After acknowledging the successful NAACP's voter registration efforts in Virginia, North Carolina, Texas, Florida, Georgia, and Louisiana, when holding African Americans responsible for meeting the goals of the NAACP's voter registration campaigns, Wilkins pointed to the success of African Americans in Louisiana in adding 151,000 voters in sixteen years.[49] He also called on African Americans and their allies to imitate those in business and industry who organized and lobbied to bend Congress, the statehouse, and even the White House to their wills. Wilkins thought that African Americans and their allies were mistaken in ceding the political arena to the titans of business and industry rather than using it to achieve their civil rights goals:

> landlords, textile manufacturers, natural gas companies, watch manufacturers, theatre proprietors, railroads, airlines, cosmetic manufacturers and a host of others do not blush at lobbying for their objectives. If it is legitimate to lobby and use political pressure to secure wider mar-

> kets and fatter profits, what is so wrong with using political power to secure human rights? The answer is, "nothing," and Negro Americans should proceed on that basis.[50]

Wilkins believed that constant agitation and unyielding pressure were the answer, and he suggested that "as long as Northern Negroes stay sweet and well-behaved, the Northern party bosses will let the South do as it pleases."[51] He drew attention to the fact that African Americans controlled the voter registration process until the point when it became public. For example, African Americans staffed their voting registration clinics, developed its curriculum, and taught its educational workshops. Often, such activities did not attract Southern whites' attention until it was time to register to vote. Unlike Strong, Wilkins believed in the power of ordinary citizens to assume the reigns of leadership, and he recognized their gift for exploiting vulnerabilities in the system by noting:

> If one or two, or a mere half dozen persons venture to the registration offices they can be "handled" easily, not necessarily physically, but psychologically. But if several hundred people line up to be registered the sheer number becomes a challenge. It is not easy for clerks to talk hundreds out of registering, nor to fail hundreds in tests. The attention of the public is attracted, discussion ensues, newspaper stories appear, political figures take note. A fact becomes demonstrated, and this demonstration is more powerful than a mere claim.[52]

Preparation and persistence were the keys to overcoming the impediments to voting at the precinct level, and Wilkins recommended a straightforward method for adding new voters: the candidates had to study until they could pass the tests then go and register to vote at the appropriate place and time.[53]

Pointing to the NAACP's recent "Prayer Pilgrimage for Freedom in Washington last May 17," Wilkins did not shield the NAACP or civil rights leaders from criticism. Approximately "twenty-five thousand people from thirty states" had attended the demonstration chanting "Give us the ballot" among other refrains. From the podium, the "Reverends C. K. Steele, Fred Shuttlesworth, Martin Luther King, Jr., Representative Adam Clayton Powell and others . . . [delivered moving speeches and called] for putting more pressure on elected officials to implement school integration and to pass civil rights legislation."[54] Despite that outpouring of support, Wilkins noted:

> We have a lot to learn about simple public relations techniques. Very often we do not have to *do* anything; we just have to *be there* in numbers to show how we feel and what we intend to do. The Prayer Pilgrimage for Freedom in Washington last May 17, was an impressive gathering in behalf of civil rights; but it could have been so much more impressive, not with more impassioned speeches, but with more thousands just being there.[55]

Six years later, Wilkins' observation would bear fruit in the 1963 March on Washington for Jobs and Freedom.

Samuel Lubell brought to the 1957 Yearbook symposium not only his command of the data but also his method for extracting larger insights from it by combining statistical analyses with face-to-face interviews in "key" precincts. When describing his method, Lubell noted: "I pick a city or precinct that reveals certain changes and I do not leave until I know why there has been a historic break with the past record."[56]

The *Journal*'s readers may have been familiar with Lubell's work through the review of *Revolt of the Moderates* in the autumn 1956 issue by political scientist Robert E. Martin. In describing that book's thesis, Martin continued:

> The author is especially concerned with the problem of political realignment in the United States, and with realistically assessing the Eisenhower Presidency. In brief summary, he is convinced that "in essence the drama of his Presidency can be described as the ordeal of a nation turned conservative and struggling—thus far with limited but precarious success—to give effective voice and force to that conservatism."[57]

Concurring with Lubell's assessment, Martin wrote: "The buoyant militancy of the New Deal and Fair Deal have given way to a quiet, and often smug, conservatism" that some had described as "full capitulation to the South" by the members of an expanding, prosperous, suburban-dwelling, middle class.[58]

In his 1957 Yearbook chapter, Lubell further refined the assessment that he had offered in *Revolt of the Moderates* basing his conclusions on an extensive analysis of the 1956 presidential election results including "the voting returns for predominately Negro wards and precincts in 86 cities, representing . . . nearly one million Negro votes."[59] In Lubell's opinion, African Americans' resentment over racial atrocities in the South outweighed their economic allegiance to the Democratic Party and cost Adlai Stevenson the White House. The significant defection of African American voters to Eisenhower was primarily a consequence of the failure of Southern Democrats, dominated by segregationists, to deliver meaningful economic and social benefits to African Americans in the region. Moreover, in the minds of many African American voters, the Democratic Party was associated with Jim Crow and racial injustice, and Lubell captured the mood of African Americans nationally when he wrote, "there were no [economic] levees to hold back the waters of racial anger."[60] Objectively, economic conditions had changed so much since 1932 that Lubell felt it was impossible to transplant the New Deal alliance between labor and African Americans to the South. He interpreted the 1956 election results as a repudiation of the NAACP strategy that anticipated that liberalism in the South would spread as labor unionization made inroads among Southern workers. In fact, Lubell demonstrated that Southern white workers often were willing to abandon the unions than disavow segregation making the lower cost of labor in South even more attractive to Northern manufacturing and industry.[61]

Moreover, this growth in conservatism spelled a death knell politically for Southern liberals and moderates, and Lubell pointed to the election losses of Senators Claude Pepper (Florida) and Frank Graham (North Carolina) as signaling that trend. In part, Pepper and Graham's defeats were the results of surges among white voters in response to the efforts to register more African Americans. Based on the indisputable movement in the South in the direction of conservatism, Lubell deemed "Liberalism in the South [to be] almost dead as a political force," and he was doubtful that "the Southern Negro vote can perform the political miracles that seem expected of it."[62] The changing political environment provided more threats than opportunities for Democrats, and racial issues were potent and divisive enough politically to drive a wedge splitting Northern and Southern Democrats to the Republican Party's advantage.[63] The 1956 presidential elections were a watershed exhibiting the first signs that the "deterioration" of the New Deal coalition was beyond repair. Characterizing the South as the Democratic Party's "exposed flank," Lubell felt that divisions among Democrats there gave the Republicans an opening for offsetting Democratic voting strongholds in Northern cities with the goal of destroying the Democratic Party "as an effective political power."[64]

Furthermore, Lubell suggested that the political realignment driven by conservatism would prove problematic for African Americans. Politically, they might find themselves isolated, alone, and without any friends. Economically dependent on the big city machines and lacking independent wealth or income, they could not afford to antagonize "the ruling powers" in the North or the South. The implications of this last issue applied to nearly all Americans in 1957 whether they realized it or not. It applied with added force to those Southern white workers who were organizing to stop desegregation in the workplace to maintain the privileges they had enjoyed under Jim Crow. Neither prescriptions for self-determination such as those offered by the NAACP or voter registration campaigns could do little in the short run to resolve this impasse for African Americans. Was it necessary for African American voters to perform the miracles expected of them, and who would benefit from their feats? Thompson did not pretend to have answers. For him, *The Negro Voter in the South* had raised the visibility of the issue, and that Yearbook would have rendered a service if such questions resonated in Afro-America and beyond for some time to come and stimulated further thought, research, organization, and activism.

NOTES

1. Charles H. Thompson, "Editorial Comment: The Dilemma of Negro Voters," *The Journal of Negro Education*, 25, no. 4 (Autumn 1956): 369.
2. Ibid., 369.
3. Ibid.
4. Ibid.
5. Ibid., 369–70, italics in original.
6. Ibid., 370.
7. Ibid.
8. Ibid.
9. Gerhard Peters and John T. Woolley, "The American Presidency Project," accessed July 9, 2017, http://www.presidency.ucsb.edu/showelection.php?year=1956.
10. Henry Lee Moon, "Editorial Comment: The Negro Vote in the Presidential Election of 1956," *The Journal of Negro Education*, 26, no. 3 (Summer 1957): 225.
11. Charles H. Thompson, "Editorial Comment: Desegregation 1956; Prospects 1957," *The Journal of Negro Education*, 26, no. 1 (Winter 1957): 2.
12. Ibid., 2.
13. Ibid.
14. Ibid., 3.
15. Ibid.
16. Ibid.
17. Ibid.
18. Ibid.
19. Please see Charles S. Johnson, "A Southern Negro's View of the South," *The Journal of Negro Education*, 26, no. 1 (Winter 1957): 4.
20. Ibid., 4.
21. Ibid., 8.
22. Ibid., 4–5.
23. Ibid., 5.
24. Ibid., 6.
25. Ibid., 8–9.
26. Ibid., 9.
27. Please see Howard Hale Long, "The Relative Learning Capacities of Negroes and Whites," *The Journal of Negro Education*, 26, no. 2 (Spring 1957): 121.
28. Charles H. Thompson, "Editorial Comment: The Gold Coast Revolution," *The Journal of Negro Education*, 26, no. 2 (Spring 1957): 97; Thompson incorrectly identified Ghana as the first African colony to gain its independence instead of the Sudan, which became independent on January 1, 1956.
29. Thompson, "The Gold Coast Revolution," 97; The African Americans in attendance as private citizens included Horace Mann Bond, Ralph Bunche, Charles Diggs, publisher John H. Johnson, Mordecai W. Johnson, Reverend Dr. Martin and Mrs. Coretta Scott King, Adam Clayton Powell, Jr., Thurgood Marshall, Roy Wilkins of the NAACP, and A. Phillip Randolph.
30. Thompson, "The Gold Coast Revolution," 97.
31. Ibid., 98.
32. Ibid.
33. Ibid.
34. Ibid.
35. Charles H. Thompson, "Editorial Comment: The Negro Voter in the South," *The Journal of Negro Education*, 26, no. 3 (Summer 1957): 215.
36. James M. Nabrit, Jr., "The Future of the Negro Voter in the South," *The Journal of Negro Education*, 26, no. 3 (Summer 1957): 422.
37. Florence B. Irving, "The Future of the Negro Voter in the South," *The Journal of Negro Education*, 26, no. 3 (Summer 1957): 390.
38. Ibid., 390.

39. Ibid., 391, 393–95.
40. Ibid., 397.
41. Ibid., 399.
42. Donald S. Strong, "The Future of the Negro Voter in the South," *The Journal of Negro Education*, 26, no. 3 (Summer 1957): 403.
43. Ibid., 405.
44. Ibid., 407.
45. James M. Nabrit, Jr., "The Future of the Negro Voter in the South," 419.
46. Ibid., 420.
47. Ibid., 423.
48. Roy Wilkins, "The Future of the Negro Voter in the United States," *The Journal of Negro Education*, 26, no. 3 (Summer 1957): 427.
49. Ibid., 426, 424.
50. Ibid., 430.
51. Ibid., 427.
52. Ibid., 426.
53. Ibid.
54. Collier-Thomas and Franklin, 64.
55. Roy Wilkins, "The Future of the Negro Voter in the United States," 426; italics in the original.
56. Richard Pearson, "Samuel Lubell, Public Opinion Analyst, Dies," *Washington Post*, August 23, 1987, accessed July 17, 2017, https://www.washingtonpost.com/archive/local/1987/08/23/samuel-lubell-public-opinion-analyst-dies/62f30632-5a61-429d-a44f-9b9e73daf264/?utm_term=.10a8eebb3164; Ronald Smothers, "Samuel Lubell is Dead at 76; Predicted Election Outcomes," *New York Times*, August 21, 1987, accessed July 17, 2017, http://www.nytimes.com/1987/08/21/obituaries/samuel-lubell-is-dead-at-76-predicted-election-outcomes.html.
57. Robert E. Martin, "The Struggle for Political Realignment: Review of *Revolt of the Moderates* by Samuel Lubell," *The Journal of Negro Education*, 25, no. 4 (Autumn 1956): 424.
58. Ibid., 424.
59. Samuel Lubell, "The Future of the Negro Voter in the United States," *The Journal of Negro Education*, 26, no. 3 (Summer 1957): 408.
60. Ibid., 408.
61. Ibid., 410.
62. Ibid., 411, 414.
63. Ibid., 416.
64. Ibid., 417.

SIX

Strengthening African American Higher Education

As a dean of the Howard University Graduate School, Thompson was, in the autumn of 1957, without the services of historian John Hope Franklin who had moved beyond Howard University northward to Brooklyn College. Thompson possessed the rare gift of commitment that was not sectarian, and rather than throwing roadblocks in Franklin's path, Thompson applauded his scholarship and service to the university as well as the national service he rendered in helping to resolve the thorny historical issues that the Supreme Court had considered when deciding *Brown I* (1954). Above all, Thompson thought that mainstream higher education needed the talents of brilliant scholars such as Franklin, and that without opportunities for cross-pollination, the entire landscape soon would become barren.

As Thompson bade farewell to some colleagues, he welcomed others into Howard University's faculty ranks, among those a teacher who was too obscure to be mentioned in the classic, *Howard University: The First Hundred Years, 1867–1967*. A 1953 graduate of Howard, Chloe Anthony Wofford (Toni Morrison) was so highly regarded by the faculty that she was hired as an instructor of English in 1957 and taught there until 1964, eventually leaving and garnering the Pulitzer Prize, and, subsequently, the Nobel Prize as a novelist of the African American experience.[1]

In his fall 1957 editorial, Thompson appraised the Civil Rights Act of 1957 recently passed by Congress and signed into law by President Eisenhower on September 9, 1957. The genesis of this legislation was a 1956 Republican Party election proposal that was designed to sharpen the divisions within the Democratic Party by stoking African Americans' disenchantment with the Democrats' tepid response to racial violence in the South, including the murders of Emmett Till and Reverend George Lee in

Mississippi. However, after securing reelection, President Eisenhower distanced himself from this aspect of his party's civil rights platform and, notably, the proposals championed by Attorney General Herbert Brownell to empower the Justice Department to hasten the desegregation process via lawsuits on behalf of African Americans in the South. While the House of Representatives adopted a Brownell inspired version of the 1957 Civil Rights Bill, the Senate passed considerably weaker legislation that was instead focused on enforcing African Americans' voting rights. The ensuing bill being only a shadow of the original, many of its supporters considered abandoning it and beginning the process anew in the next session of Congress. On the contrary, the National Association for the Advancement of Colored People was among those opposed to rewriting the bill and its leadership "urged acceptance of the bill because, while it was not satisfactory . . . it was thought to be wiser to accept what could be got now and work for amendments later." In a similar vein, the Eisenhower administration promoted the Senate Bill as "a decided gain" that substantially strengthened civil rights protections.[2]

Although the bill enlarged the franchise for African Americans, Thompson did not regard voting as a panacea; in fact, he thought that voting would do little to relieve the injustice that African Americans were experiencing in the South. According to Thompson, registering more African American voters would neither materially change African Americans' status nor reduce the widening racial gap in median income even in cities such as Washington, DC, where African Americans' prospects for employment were greater than elsewhere in the nation. Indeed, Thompson believed that freedom "from discrimination in employment or . . . from economic reprisals" was of more consequence, that civil rights legislation that lacked such protections would have mostly symbolic value, and that "the most serious and critical disadvantage which Negroes suffer at present is economic, and much, if not most, of it is due to race."[3] Nonetheless, like other critics of the bill who were in agreement with the National Association for the Advancement of Colored People, Thompson noted, "those who insist that the current bill is only a first step in the direction of securing civil rights for Negroes are undoubtedly correct. It is our hope that they will make every effort to see that this first step is immediately followed by others which will more realistically meet the Negro's civil rights problem."[4]

The December 5, 1957, annual meeting of the Southern Association of Colleges and Secondary Schools, the regional accreditation agency for much of the South, shifted Thompson's gaze once more to African American higher education. By voice vote, the members present approved the admission of fifteen African American senior colleges and three junior colleges to full membership in the Southern Association, based on the same standards the association applied to white colleges in the region. The Southern Association also maintained eight African

American colleges on its "Approved List of Colleges for Negro Youth without Notation," because they "seemed closer to membership than others at the moment."[5] In his winter 1958 editorial "The Southern Association and Negro College Membership," Thompson printed a portion of the Southern Association's press release announcing the admission of these African American colleges to membership, noting that the association had been evaluating the African American colleges in its region for more than twenty years. According to this document, in the "late thirties," the Association had assigned one of its committees the task of "helping the [African American colleges] meet the same standards as the Association required" of white colleges in the region. Moreover:

> In 1951, when the Association felt that these schools were nearing the minimum excellence required of its members, [the Southern Association secured a grant] from the General Education Board to make an exhaustive study of each of the sixty-three colleges for Negro youth. These studies have continued since that date, and the action just taken [to admit qualified African American colleges to full membership] is a recognition of the educational achievement of these Negro institutions.[6]

This report puzzled Thompson in that it implied that no African American college had met the association's standards "(except that of being white)" before 1951, and he also pointed out that before December 5, 1957, the association "had not put itself on record" as equating the college education offered by an accredited African American college with that provided by an accredited white college. "Whatever may be the reasons which account for the unfortunate implications of this news release, the action of the Association needs to be put in proper historical perspective," Thompson asserted.[7]

He further recalled that thirty years earlier, the "old Association for Colleges for Negro Youth" had unsuccessfully approached the Southern Association several times for evaluation of the African American colleges for accreditation purposes. Subsequently it "persuaded the U. S. Bureau of Education to make a survey of Negro colleges," resulting in the Klein Survey (1928) which in turn led the members of the Association for Colleges for Negro Youth to "[debate] and [veto] the proposition" of evaluating themselves and decide to approach the Southern Association once more. This latter request met with the Southern Association's interest but although it agreed to conduct accreditation inspections, the Southern Association refused to grant any African American college membership that would include the privilege of attending meetings, for such inclusion was taboo during segregation. Therefore, Thompson asserted, "In every other respect the Negro colleges, in order to be given unconditional accreditation, were supposed to meet in full all the standards which the white colleges were required to meet."[8]

This first evaluation process began in 1930, with the association adopting a two-tiered rating system over the objections of African American educators such as Thompson who desired a single set of accreditation standards. Under this rubric, the association assigned an "A" to any African American college meeting the same standards as the four-year white colleges in the region and a "B" to those failing to meet one or more of these standards: only one senior African American college received an A rating in 1930, and two others did so in the following year. By 1932, six African American senior colleges had earned an A rating and twenty-two others the B rating; by 1952, the Southern Association listed fifty-two "fully approved" African American colleges, and, noted in its December 1957 press release that it had discontinued the two-tiered rating system "several years earlier."[9]

The Southern Association's December 1957 press release also suggested that the African American colleges were "nearing the minimum standards required of its members, [in 1951]" which Thompson found disconcerting. Equally perplexing to him was the decision of the Southern Association to obtain funding for "an exhaustive [five-year] study of each of the sixty-three colleges for Negro youth" in its region: if the fifty-two African American colleges were "fully approved" in 1952 but not in 1957, did that mean that the association had not applied the same standards in 1952 as it applied the white colleges in the region, despite its assurances to the contrary? Alternatively, Thompson wondered whether the African American colleges in the South "had deteriorated to such an extent that a special study had to be made of *each* of them. In any case, it would have been enlightening if it had been noted why this apparently unusual procedure was instituted."[10]

Nonetheless, Thompson reported that the Southern Association planned to discontinue its "separate list of Colleges for Negro Youth" in 1961 and deny regional accreditation to any African American college that failed to meet one or more of its standards beyond that date. Despite wondering why the association had not accredited any African American secondary schools in December 1957, Thompson regarded the decision to admit eighteen African American colleges to full membership in the Southern Association as "historic." The development had taken twenty-seven years, and Thompson felt that this achievement was also noteworthy because "[it represented] the beginning of the end of an anomalous situation whose correction has been long overdue. We wish to congratulate the Association for taking this forward step in spite of the difficulties involved."[11]

In the spring and summer of 1958, Thompson's gaze remained fixed on the implications of the Southern Association's decision to apply uniform accreditation standards to all colleges in the South. This concern was the focus of his speech, "The Negro College: In Retrospect and Prospect," delivered in Richmond, Virginia, at Virginia Union University on

November 12 or 13, 1957, at an academic convocation commemorating the American Baptist Home Missionary Society's 125th anniversary. Thompson published this paper and several other addresses featured at the convocation in the *Journal*'s spring 1958 issue, and in his spring 1958 editorial, "The 125th Anniversary of the American Baptist Home Mission Society," introducing those commentaries, he celebrated the vision, courage, and tenacity of the leaders of the benevolent societies that had founded African American colleges during Reconstruction, considering these leaders' work among the most important legacies of that tumultuous period.

Unlike the builders of the munificent mansions erected during the Gilded Age, the northern missionaries and the ex-slaves who founded institutions of learning looked to their colleges as a means of satisfying African Americans' thirst for education and their need to carve out a niche in US society. By 1867, Thompson noted, officials with the Freedmen's Bureau had estimated that nearly one million African American children were not in school for want of some twenty thousand teachers. Realizing that all the white teachers from the South and the North combined could not fill more than "a few thousand" of these vacancies, they concluded that training African Americans to serve as teachers was the only feasible solution. Moreover, this need to provide teachers for nearly four million ex-slaves added a sense of urgency to the drive to build African American colleges in the South. Thus, Thompson characterized African American higher education in the South as a logical response to the exigencies of war and the need to rebuild Southern society rather than a luxury or a travesty. In the spring of 1958, he concluded that not only had the African American college graduates made public education for African Americans in the South possible, but that the colleges:

> indicated in a most unmistakable and striking way that the ceiling of Negro ambition was not to be limited by his status at that time nor his previous condition. There must be not only Negro teachers, said the officials of the societies working in the field of Negro uplift, but also leaders in all areas of Negro life. Hence, they concluded, that there must be higher institutions which would be centers of training and leadership for the whole Negro race.[12]

While it was true that "Negroes have never ceased to be grateful to the organizations which exhibited faith in those dark days and acted upon it," it also was true in the spring of 1958 that African American higher education had reached a crossroads.[13] Desegregation had ushered in a new set of challenges that not only questioned the rationale of the African American colleges but also tested their sustainability. In "The Negro College: in Retrospect and Prospect," the speech he delivered in November 1957, Thompson asked a series of questions that he believed that the leaders of African American higher education had avoided, to the detriment of their institutions. Among these were:

> What effect is desegregation having, or is likely to have, upon the formerly segregated Negro college—public and private? What, if any, plans have been made, or are being contemplated by the Negro college, in the light of the theory and fact of desegregation? What, if any, changes in philosophy, objectives, or program are being contemplated, or seem desirable [to equip the African American college for its new role and responsibilities?][14]

Thompson used these concerns to preview the 1958 issue of the Yearbook, *Desegregation and the Negro College,* whose purpose was to provoke African American educators to "come to grips" with the realities of desegregation because it was apparent to him that desegregation had notably altered the educational landscape in African American higher education in theory if not also in fact.

Desegregation had authored the introductory chapter in a new era of competition that would challenge the most competitive African American colleges while making the elimination of lesser institutions inevitable. Abundant data was available from sources such as *Southern School News,* and yet Thompson found that critical evaluations of these data were not only difficult to obtain but virtually nonexistent. He noted that the 1948 issue of the Yearbook, *Negro Higher and Professional Education in the United States,* was ten years old and that in the interim much had changed in US higher education, including several landmark rulings by the Supreme Court in *Sipuel v. Board of Regents of the University of Oklahoma* (1948), *Sweatt v. Painter* (1950), and *McLaurin v. Oklahoma State Regents* (1950). The rulings in *Sweatt* and *McLaurin* had come within a hair of declaring racial segregation in higher education unconstitutional, and now that the *Brown* decision had ushered in the era of desegregation, Thompson felt that an up-to-date survey of African American higher education was required.

To test this hypothesis, Thompson did some basic research using contemporaneous sources, but he encountered difficulty in answering straightforward questions and found it next to impossible to obtain coherent research related to desegregation. To address those deficiencies, Thompson published the 1958 Yearbook, *Desegregation and the Negro College,* to provide a comprehensive overview of the status of desegregation in higher education in the seventeen states and the District of Columbia where racial segregation had been mandatory. Moreover, he planned this Yearbook to identify the threats and opportunities that desegregation posed to African American colleges nationally.

Thompson planned *Desegregation and the Negro College* to comprise twenty-five chapters divided into three sections. The first part provided a historical overview of the development of African American higher education in the United States with an emphasis on the South in order to evaluate proposals concerning the future directions that these colleges might explore. The second part was intended to gauge "The Present Status of Desegregation in Higher Education in the South," based on data from eleven states and the nation's capital where some desegregation in higher education had occurred. For this section, Thompson obtained essays from educators who were close to the local scenes in Arkansas, Delaware, Kentucky, Maryland, Missouri, Oklahoma, Tennessee, and West Virginia, and from states that were hotbeds of resistance in 1958 such as Louisiana, North Carolina, and Virginia. To complete this section of the 1958 Yearbook, Thompson recruited economist Brailsford R. Brazeal, an expert on fair employment practices and a citizen of Georgia, to give a detailed account of the status of desegregation in higher education in Alabama, Florida, Georgia, Mississippi, and South Carolina. The third section consisted of an essay-based symposium capped by critical summaries by Martin D. Jenkins, president of Morgan State College in Baltimore, Maryland, who had worked closely with Thompson at Howard University and regarded him as his mentor, and Guy B. Johnson, the University of North Carolina's noted professor of sociology and anthropology, who was a highly visible Southern white moderate also serving as a trustee of Howard University.

The Yearbook also contained four indices summing up the issues confronting the leaders of African American higher education in 1958, the major indicators in descending order being accreditation, endowment, enrollment, and denominational affiliation. Anyone who could interpret those markers could predict the future of a given college or university with a fair amount of accuracy, and although anyone who had access to accurate data and was willing to face its implications could have done the same, such information was often inaccessible even for college presidents or trustees. In fact, the lack of such data was very probably a sign that a given college's survival was doubtful.

World War II had represented a turning point in African American higher education, according to Stephen J. Wright, president of Fisk University, and another protégé of Thompson's. In the academic year 1940/1941, the enrollment in the South's African American private and public colleges had split evenly: 20,270 students attended the private colleges and 19,583 students the public colleges. By the academic year 1956/1957, African American public colleges dominated this part of the higher education sector, enrolling 44,752 students in contrast to the 30,111 students attending African American private colleges: whereas there was an overall increase in enrollment, the gain was nearly three times as large for the public institutions. Over the years, African American public colleges had become increasingly strong in terms of academics while providing access to higher education at significantly lower costs than African American private institutions. When recruiting new faculty or adding new facilities or programs, African American public colleges could turn to their state legislatures for resources and support. And yet, in 1958 "the private Negro colleges [were] the lowest-cost colleges of the private college group in America," according to Frederick D. Patterson, president of the Phelps Stokes Fund, and William J. Trent, Jr., executive director of the United Negro College Fund.[15] Because students from low-income families filled their classrooms and dormitories, the presidents of African American private colleges often walked a tightrope between providing quality instruction and keeping the cost of tuition, room, and board low enough to attract the numbers of students required for their colleges to stay afloat.

Wright reported that of the sixty African American private colleges in the South in 1958, nearly 83 percent had affiliations with a religious denomination. Because several religious denominations had founded more African American colleges during Reconstruction than they could maintain adequately in 1958, the Baptists, Methodists, and African Methodist Episcopalians having respectively founded twelve, ten, and seven private colleges in the South, these groups controlled twenty-nine of the thirty-seven institutions at risk of losing accreditation from the Southern Association. Moreover, the African American church-related colleges often lacked the steady cash flow necessary for fending off threats or for exploiting opportunities because they depended on donations collected weekly from various congregations for a portion of their operating revenue. Patterson and Trent reported in 1958 that despite their glorious history, the American Baptist Home Mission Society and its Board of Education and the African Methodist Episcopal Church were guilty of providing merely "token support to the colleges which they [had] founded."[16] While a constant preoccupation with raising money for operating expenses was not a prescription for sound management, in Wright's estimation, senseless feuds and rivalries often distracted the various denominational boards from closing, consolidating, or relocating the private colleges in order to bolster their enrollment or increase their chances of survival.

In addition to these, financial constraints in the strengthened accreditation standards had transformed the environment of African American higher education, placing the church-related colleges at a competitive disadvantage. Elaborating on this theme, Wright noted that the Southern Association required colleges enrolling three hundred students or fewer to have at least forty thousand dollars in fixed income with "not less than $12,000 [of its fixed income] to be earned from an endowment of not less than $300,000." Consequently, Wright predicted that twenty-two African American church-related colleges would lose regional accreditation in 1961 because they lacked the money for meeting several accreditation standards.[17]

Concurring with Wright's assessment, Patterson and Trent reported that even when combined, the colleges in the United Negro College Fund had less money in endowment trusts than Northwestern University did in 1958. They pointed out that only four of the thirty-three colleges comprising the United Negro College Fund had endowments of five million dollars or higher in 1958, ten colleges had reasonable prospects of success, having endowments that ranged between one million and five million dollars; six colleges were near the tipping point, each having between fifty thousand and one million dollars in endowments. Moreover, thirteen colleges were at risk because they were near "or below the requirements [for an endowment] as set forth by the Southern Association of Colleges and Secondary Schools."[18]

In his essay, "The Future of the Desegregated Negro College," Martin D. Jenkins challenged Wright for equating selective admissions standards with institutional survival. Debunking Wright's thesis, Jenkins argued that for most of the colleges under discussion, selective admissions standards were just "not attainable." Boutique educational programs were not only expensive but required distinguished faculty, and Jenkins thought it unlikely that the economic prospects of African Americans would produce enough students who could opt for quality over price in the foreseeable future, whereas higher admissions standards would function to lower the educational opportunity afforded to "the lower ranking applicants." An expert in testing, Jenkins also questioned the use of "the usual standard tests [with] low validity for use with Negro groups [or using] high school rank" as sound criteria for selecting gifted students.[19]

Another problem facing African American higher education, Jenkins and S. M. Nabrit pointed out, was the added cost associated with remedying the defects of the inadequate preparation that many of their students had received in high school. While African American colleges might be required to give their students the support that many of them needed to succeed, Jenkins also believed that fulfilling the spirit of desegregation required a commitment to sound academic standards. According to Jenkins:

> The Negro college has an especial obligation to bring students to an understanding of their role in a desegregating society. This includes a real appreciation of their responsibilities and opportunities. But it involves a great deal more than this. It means that the college must raise its expectation of the level of student accomplishment; that it must eliminate those students who do not meet minimum levels of performance, even though this may have an adverse effect on overall enrollment.[20]

He advised college leaders to maintain a strong *esprit de corps* while shifting resources from "fraternal, athletic and other extra-classroom activities" in order to strengthen curriculum and instruction. In addition to internships and opportunities for service learning, Jenkins envisioned these colleges providing opportunities for students to experience living in a non-segregated society and in developing relationships across racial lines. Because so many of their students were academically underprepared, Jenkins felt that most African American colleges should reduce their curricular offerings while making wiser use of facilities, and eliminating graduate courses and boutique programming that enrolled only a few students. In Jenkins' opinion, it was within reach of most African American colleges, public and private, to provide quality instruction in the liberal arts and teacher training. Over time, he believed, the state boards of education would concentrate specialized or graduate offerings in "agriculture, home economics, and law" at "flagship" universities, thereby lessening the need for the African American land-grant colleges to provide those services.[21]

As a college president in the University of Maryland system that had desegregated recently, Jenkins advised his readers that this process was not free-of-risk with many supporting the complete elimination of "Negro administrators and teachers and a reduction in appropriations." Old fashioned political organization, lobbying, and voting as an interest group were the solution to this problem, according to Jenkins who thought that "desegregation need not result in loss of opportunity for well-qualified Negro administrators and teachers."[22]

To deal with desegregation and other challenges, it was imperative for the leaders of African American higher education and their boards to engage in self-study and planning related to defining their institution's future role and program regarding not only desegregation, but also "all the other factors commonly considered by colleges in projecting their programs."[23] One of the highlights of Jenkins' chapter was his warning to the African American private colleges against entering into partnerships with the Southern states:

> Perhaps the major imperative for maintaining the private Negro college in the South is to assure the existence of institutions which are in large measure free of state control. Once the colleges become dependent upon state appropriations for their support, [their independence would be lost.][24]

Several contributors to the 1958 Yearbook felt that desegregation would have little effect on most African American colleges for at least another decade. In fact, Guy B. Johnson thought that court-ordered desegregation would strengthen state support for educational equalization campaigns as many Southern states chose to expand their public historically black colleges and universities in the hope of delaying the implementation of integration for as long as possible. Accreditation was an entirely different matter, and Johnson foresaw this process wreaking havoc upon the smaller African American private colleges in the region. In the absence of a "depression or a major war," the demand for higher education in the South was likely to remain high and require the services of every decent college, regardless of its racial composition. Nonetheless, Johnson argued that few Southern whites would attend a historically black college or university unless this institution enjoyed a strong local or regional reputation, few other options for higher education existed in that locality, or other options were oversubscribed.[25]

If the South had been "let alone," in "even the most liberal of the border states," Southern whites would have postponed desegregation until 1964 or even 1974, Guy Johnson acknowledged.[26] He took comfort in the fact that twelve Southern states and the District of Columbia accounted for 248 of the 252 colleges and 45 percent of the institutions of higher learning in those states that had desegregated. When viewed from the perspective of student enrollment, very little desegregation in higher education had actually occurred in the region: for example, during the regular academic year, five thousand African American students (5 percent of the nationwide African American student enrollment) attended previously white colleges in the South. However, their enrollment at the previously white 248 campuses ranged from one student to 150 students. Moreover, approximately twelve hundred African American students attended desegregated institutions resulting from the consolidation of teachers' colleges in Louisville, Kentucky; Washington, DC; and St. Louis, Missouri.[27] Guy B. Johnson therefore described desegregation as a one-way street involving the enrollment of African American students in previously all-white colleges, concurring with the late Charles S. Johnson that it was more accurate in 1958 to speak of "several Souths. The Border States are behaving perhaps a little better, the Deep South states a little worse, than we might have expected ten years ago. Certainly, the pace of change with regard to racial patterns is already strikingly different in these two sections."[28] Guy B. Johnson also believed that white racism and African Americans' self-interest would combine to ensure the preservation of African American higher education. An astute student of the South and human relations, he "strongly suspected" that:

> many Negro educational leaders during the next twenty-five years will be . . . trying to keep their institutions from losing their racial identity completely [by covertly facilitating] the white group's interest in holding desegregation to the slowest possible pace.[29]

Jenkins, on the other hand, questioned the legitimacy of race-based institutions, an assumption receiving "little attention" in *Desegregation and the Negro College* that led him, near the conclusion of his essay, to cite an observation made by Felton G. Clark in his 1958 Yearbook essay, "The Development and Present Status of Publicly-Supported Higher Education for Negroes":

> the interesting challenge [is] to become American institutions rather than institutions for a special group. This suggests that their programs should be oriented in terms of the goals of the American college. High-

> er educational institutions for Negroes should be concerned with helping youth to acquire the outlook, skills, and knowledge for effective living as members of the American economy; with helping youth to develop a value system consistent with the democratic creed; and with providing an educational climate that stresses competition with standards of excellence.[30]

In the remaining years of his editorship, Thompson's concern for African American higher education would manifest itself through the publication of a Yearbook in 1960 and another Yearbook in 1962 that updated the relevant research and gave his readers access to diverse, often sharply conflicting, perspectives. As dean of the Graduate School at Howard University, Thompson had anticipated some of the debate featured in *Desegregation and the Negro College*. In December 1954, Thompson had cast the tie-breaking vote in the Graduate Council that cleared the way for Howard University to offer instruction leading to the PhD. While *Desegregation and the Negro College* was in press, on June 6, 1958, Howard University awarded its first doctoral degrees in chemistry, and Thompson conferred PhD degrees in chemistry on Howard Delaney and Bibhuti Mazumder at the university's commencement exercises on June 6, 1958.[31] During much of the postwar period, desegregation remained at the top of Thompson's policy agenda. With the publication of *Desegregation and the Negro College,* Thompson had focused his readers' and concerned policymakers' attention on the one problem capable of closing nearly 25 percent of the African American colleges in the South, upending one of the most important legacies of Reconstruction.

NOTES

1. Magalit Fox, "Toni Morrison, Towering Novelist of the Black Experience, Dies at 88," *New York Times,* August 6, 2019, accessed on August 6, 2019, https://www.nytimes.com/2019/08/06/books/toni-morrison-dead.html.
2. Charles H. Thompson, "Editorial Comment: The Civil Rights Bill of 1957," *The Journal of Negro Education,* 26, no. 4 (Autumn 1957): 433.
3. Charles H. Thompson, "The Civil Rights Bill of 1957," 434.
4. Ibid.
5. Charles H. Thompson, "Editorial Comment: The Southern Association and Negro College Membership," *The Journal of Negro Education,* 27, no. 1 (Winter 1958): 1.
6. Ibid., 1.
7. Ibid., 2.
8. Ibid., 2.
9. Ibid.
10. Ibid., 3.
11. Ibid.
12. Charles H. Thompson, "Editorial Comment: The 125th Anniversary of the American Baptist Home Mission Society," *The Journal of Negro Education,* 27, no. 2 (Spring 1958): 101.
13. Ibid., 102.

14. Charles H. Thompson, "The Negro College: In Retrospect and in Prospect," *The Journal of Negro Education*, 27, no. 2 (Spring 1958): 128.
15. W. J. Trent, Jr., and F. D. Patterson, "Financial Support of the Private Negro College," *The Journal of Negro Education*, 27, no. 3 (Summer 1958): 398.
16. Ibid., 399.
17. Stephen J. Wright, "The Future of the Negro Private College: Philosophy and Program," *The Journal of Negro Education*, 27, no. 3 (Summer 1958): 407–8.
18. Trent and Patterson, "Financial Support," 401.
19. Martin D. Jenkins, "The Future of the Desegregated Negro College: A Critical Summary," *The Journal of Negro Education*, 27, no. 3 (Summer 1958): 425, 427–28.
20. Ibid., 428.
21. Ibid., 422–23.
22. Ibid., 423.
23. Ibid., 426.
24. Ibid., 424.
25. Guy B. Johnson, "Desegregation and the Future of the Negro College: A Critical Summary," *The Journal of Negro Education*, 27, no. 3 (Summer 1958): 434.
26. Ibid., 432.
27. Ibid., 430–31.
28. Ibid., 433.
29. Ibid.
30. Felton G. Clark, "The Development and Present Status of Publicly-Supported Higher Education of Negroes," *The Journal of Negro Education*, 27, no. 3 (Summer 1958): 232, quoted in Jenkins, "The Future of the Desegregated Negro College," 428–29.
31. Logan, *Howard University: The First Hundred Years, 1867–1967*, 419–20.

SEVEN

The Criminalization of African American Youth

In his autumn 1958 editorial, "With All Deliberate Speed," Thompson focused his analysis on the Court's most notable ruling after *Brown I* (1954), basing it on his reading and rumination at the end of that September. In addition to offering a critique of *Cooper v. Aaron* (1958), Thompson reprinted the text of that decision in the autumn 1958 issue of the *Journal*'s "Current Trends in Negro Education and Shorter Papers" section. *Cooper v. Aaron* was concerned with the resistance surrounding the desegregation of Central High School in Little Rock, Arkansas, that had prompted President Eisenhower to intervene by nationalizing the Arkansas National Guard to ensure that court-ordered school desegregation could proceed peacefully. The "immediate issue" raised by this case was whether public opposition to desegregation, including mob violence, was a justifiable reason for granting the Little Rock Independent School Board's request to delay court-ordered desegregation by more than two years. For Thompson, the real issue in the case was the Court's seriousness about enforcing the standard of "with all deliberate speed" that it had established in *Brown II* to assess good faith compliance with the desegregation of public education. In this decision, the Court had unanimously upheld the principle that it had articulated in *Brown I* despite the addition of three new justices and serving as the target of "the most demagogic vilification" in seventy-five years, and sustained that precedent even in the face of public criticism by Eisenhower recommending that it take a "slower" approach to school desegregation. The editorial "With All Deliberate Speed" put the clarity of Thompson's reasoning on display: in two pages, he summarized the main points of the Court's decision, including its forcible assertion of its primacy in deciding the law of the land. The Court's position on mob violence was keenly awaited by supporters and detractors of the *Brown* decision: if the Court had agreed with the Little Rock school district, it would have sent an open invitation to those wishing to maintain school segregation through a show of force. If the Court had wavered or retreated in the slightest, it would have set back the desegregation movement by "at least 50 years" and negate in a single stroke the quarter-century spent in establishing desegregation as an accepted principle in law.[1] Thompson refused to criticize the Court or debate whether the evidence suggested that the Little Rock Independent School Board had demonstrated good faith through its limited and class-based approach to desegregating public education. Instead, he praised the willingness of the justices to look beyond the issues at hand in order to anticipate and rule emphatically in the negative on the question of whether it was possible to maintain segregation in public education by resorting to privatization. Although Thompson was confident that the supporters of segregation would develop additional schemes for delaying school desegregation, he took comfort from the fact that the Court had declared in *Cooper v. Aaron* that "with all deliberate speed" was not code for the abandonment of desegregation.[2]

In the winter 1959 issue of the *Journal*, Thompson's concern shifted to the moral issues underlying school desegregation that had received much less attention than he thought that they deserved. "The Moral Issue in Desegregation" first noted that the crisis over desegregation was not about politics, state's rights, the need to preserve law and order, or protecting the federal Constitution. On the contrary, he stated, every intelligent person in the United States understood that the real issue was whether compulsory racial segregation was morally defensible. Thompson noted that "some 19 national church bodies and seven church councils in as many Southern states" had issued statements in support of the *Brown* decision after May 17, 1954. Even more encouraging were the statements that religious leaders had issued between 1956 and 1959 not only supporting desegregation but also condemning racial segregation and calling for its elimination. One example that Thompson cited was the May 1958 declaration that "the 98th General Assembly of the Presbyterian Church in the US (Southern) opposed the use of church facilities in efforts designed to evade desegregation rulings" because denying people their civil rights because of race, color, or social class was against Christian principles.[3]

Moreover, the editors of the student newspaper at Wake Forest University and the evangelist Billy Graham were among the Southern whites who had declared that segregation was unethical. "Discrimination and the Christian Conscience," a statement issued by the Catholic bishops of the United States after its mid-November 1958 meeting, was a forthright statement condemning segregation: to the rhetorical question, "Can enforced segregation be reconciled with the Christian view of our fellowman?" this statement had asserted:

> In our judgment it cannot . . . [because] legal segregation, or any form of compulsory segregation, in itself and by its very nature imposes a stigma of inferiority upon the segregated. . . . Responsible and sober-minded Americans of all religious faiths, in all areas of our land, [must] seize the mantle of leadership from the agitator and the racist. . . . For the welfare of our Nation, we call upon all to root out from their hearts bitterness and hatred.[4]

The bishops also encouraged people to "act now and act decisively" by focusing on and implementing practical "remedies and reforms." Concurring, Thompson suggested that winter 1959 was a good time to rid the nation of the evils of segregation, and he concluded this editorial with the hope that the fundamental moral issues at the heart of the desegregation controversy would soon hold sway.[5]

The new year was barely underway before another controversy over desegregation erupted, this time by means of a news broadcast where National Broadcasting Company (NBC) news commentator Chet Huntley suggested in the "editorial summation" of his hour-long news special, "The Second Agony of Atlanta," on Sunday, February 1, 1959, that African Americans stop relying "on the courts and the federal power," predicting that white resistance would disappear opening, a space for Southern moderates to negotiate the details for advancing school desegregation in the South.[6]

The response to this assertion was so overwhelmingly in support of the National Association for the Advancement of Colored People's (NAACP's) position that NBC executives offered to broadcast a program on the following Sunday in which a "die-hard segregationist," the NAACP, and Huntley would each receive ten minutes to explain their various positions. In the *Journal*'s spring 1959 editorial, "Mr. Huntley's Astounding Proposal," Thompson focused on this second broadcast, noting:

> on February [9], 1959, the program was telecast, with Mr. Huntley as moderator, Thomas Waring, Editor of the Charleston (S.C.) *News and Courier*, to present the side of unyielding segregation, and Roy Wilkins, Executive Secretary of the NAACP, to answer Mr. Huntley's "sweeping assertion," as well as rebut the anticipated calumnies of Mr. Waring—all within the space of ten minutes.[7]

Thompson reported that Waring wanted the NAACP to cease litigation over desegregation because Southern whites would not accept any form of desegregation at any time and spent the bulk of his segment vilifying the NAACP and making derogatory comments about African Americans.[8] When his turn came, Wilkins rebutted Waring's charges that the NAACP was a communist organization by citing comments published by J. Edgar Hoover, then the director of the Federal Bureau of Investigation, that vouched for the NAACP's record of anti-communism.

Next, Wilkins challenged Huntley's assertions that the NAACP's perceived extremism was an obstacle to advancing desegregation in the Southern states, recalling that five days after the announcement of the *Brown* decision, the NAACP had cautioned its state chapter leaders against driving "hard bargains or [imposing] unnecessary hardships upon those responsible for working out the details" of desegregation. Indeed, Wilkins pointed out, the NAACP's "very first act" was to attempt compromise and to negotiate agreements about the scope and pace of desegregation, but had its overtures been not only rebuffed, but newspapers such as Waring's had printed "the names and addresses" of the NAACP members petitioning for desegregation with the "consequence [that] individual petitioners lost their jobs, were denied credit, had their mortgages foreclosed, and were in some cases driven out." Thus, Wilkins concluded, if it was extremist to "believe in the law, in the Constitution, in the courts of the nation," then African Americans and NAACP members and supporters were extremists.[9] Countering Huntley's suggestion that the NAACP did not represent African Americans in the South, Wilkins pointed out that "The Reverend Dr. Martin Luther King of Montgomery, Alabama, the National Urban League, the Negro church and the Negro press [were] unequivocal [supporters of] the NAACP." Wilkins also reminded Huntley and the television viewing audience that there were no African Americans in the state legislatures of the South and that not a single African American had voted to give the various states the authority to close the public schools.[10] African Americans also could not be blamed for any of the bombings, arson, or other forms of lawlessness and violence that plagued the South; instead, they were the victims of such premeditated violence that Southern whites had instigated. Asking African Americans to "renounce their constitutional rights, and the redress of their grievances in the courts, . . . is more than anyone has a right to ask of a people. It amounts to a request that we and our children sit by the side of the road while others zoom past us into the space age."[11] Concluding his segment Wilkins quoted Charles L. Black, a Texan on the Yale Law School faculty who had noted:

> Every thoughtful American with a spark of fair play in his veins (and this includes thousands of white people in the Deep South) wants this issue settled in justice under law. Any other method would betray not merely Negro citizens, but the moral giant that is America, our country, man's best hope for a free life in this mid-century's fresh threats of dark dictatorship.[12]

In the editorial, Thompson found Huntley unfair in equating the NAACP with the lawlessness of the White Citizens' Councils and other pro-segregationists and faulted him for having nothing more constructive to offer than proposing that African Americans surrender their rights so that the authors of violence and lawlessness might freely continue to practice white supremacy.

In a sense, the underlying theme of Thompson's project was the provision of equal educational opportunity in ways that ensured the physical, psychological, and spiritual well-being of youth in the United States, especially those from underprivileged backgrounds. To that end, Thompson designed the summer 1959 issue of the Yearbook to examine juvenile delinquency and the interaction of African American youth with the criminal justice system. By the spring of 1959, most commentators agreed that juvenile delinquency was a social problem that affected increasing numbers of youth in the United States, especially African American teenagers and youth from minority group backgrounds. Almost two decades had passed since the release of *The Negro Adolescent and His Education*, the 1940 issue of the Yearbook, and a decade since the publication of *The Negro Child in the American Social Order*, its 1950 issue. In the nineteen years between 1940 and 1959, the policing of youth had changed profoundly in the United States, and Thompson felt that an in-depth examination in the Yearbook would offer a useful resource for the investigators who were preparing for the Sixth White House Conference on Children and Youth (1960). Accordingly, his summer 1959 editorial, "Juvenile Delinquency among Negroes in the United States," addressed juvenile delinquency "one of the most critical domestic problems" confronting the country.

Thompson reported that "Juvenile arrests [had] increased two and a half times as rapidly as the youth population" and that 3 percent of juvenile delinquency involved crimes against property. However, he noted, this data omitted the youngsters living in violent, unsafe, or stressful conditions that increased the risk of their committing crimes. He deemed the data not only problematic, but lacking in standardization in terms of "the legal definitions of juvenile delinquency," for example.[13]

In the mid-1950s, the police apprehended approximately two million youth a year, but dismissed the charges against nearly 75 percent of them through a process known as "station adjustment," which involved counseling the remaining five hundred thousand youth entering the juvenile delinquency system upon their arrest and referral to juvenile court.[14] Thompson described juvenile delinquency as encompassing at least a "score or more different types of behavior and conditions," and because it was rare for the data to be disaggregated beyond broad categories such as race, gender, class, or ethnicity, clinicians and researchers could not distinguish "cases of delinquency and neglect" from those involving criminality. Accordingly, juvenile delinquency was usually considered in terms of a positive association with low-income status, with police arresting larger numbers of working-class whites and "immigrant white groups" than middle-class or upper-middle class whites, and the latter being more likely to benefit from that abovementioned "station adjustment."[15]

When it came to "the apparent rate of criminal behavior among Negroes," it was held to be "one-and-a-half to two-and-a-half times as high as that of the population as a whole," although very little research measured the extent of juvenile delinquency in African American youth or its effects on their development and social outcomes. Thus, when designing *Juvenile Delinquency among Negroes in the United States*, Thompson did *not* assume "that there is anything *inherently* peculiar about Negro youth which does not characterize the youth population as a whole,"[16] but the disproportionately high rates of arrest of African American youth *and* the lack of valid research for understanding, reducing delinquency or preventing it, prompted him to focus the 1959 Yearbook on four major topics.

The goal of the Yearbook's first section was to provide background information for understanding juvenile delinquency, with the second examining the factors associated with the high incidence of misconduct reported among African American youth. The third part presented a typology of the social agencies active in the field, and the fourth offered a critical evaluation of the various approaches to preventing or reducing delinquency in African American youth in the late 1950s.

The *Annals'* March 1959 issue focused on the prevention of juvenile delinquency, with an emphasis on empirical research into individual or community-based interventions, whereas the 1959 Yearbook relied largely on critical evaluations and syntheses of the literature and critical reflections on the researchers' or practitioners' experiences. The Yearbook also examined the effect of racial segregation and caste on juvenile delinquency and offered a measure of coherence to the contributors' efforts at identifying promising solutions for reducing delinquency among African American youth.

For nearly thirty years, Sophia Robison had done pioneering research on the ways in which social and class biases could skew the data on juvenile delinquency. In the 1930s and 1940s, she had broken new ground by showing how "race, class, ethnic group, and neighborhood of the child" served to either increase or decrease the probability that children would be labeled as juvenile delinquents. Convinced that "social research carried the obligation to help correct the problems studied," she pursued a "graduate certificate in social work at the New York School of Social Work (now the Columbia University School of Social Work)" and after achieving this in 1929 a doctorate in sociology at Columbia in 1936. After holding several leadership positions in agencies that focused on juvenile delinquency, Robison taught at the New York School of Social Work as a professor of research from 1946 until her retirement in 1954, also serving as a "consultant on juvenile delinquency to the Mid-Century White House Conference" in 1950. A prolific author, Robison published, "twelve research monographs, seven books, twenty-five publications in scholarly journals, and many reviews and papers" during her lifetime.[17]

Robison believed that "all social behavior is *learned* behavior, [reflecting] the environment in which it occurs," so that African American children (or white children, for that matter) were more likely to be labeled as delinquent when their responses to situations that they perceived as threatening differed markedly from the responses typical of white middle-class children. Moreover, because White Anglo-Saxon and Protestant values and cultural biases were often embedded in the design and the standard operating procedures of delinquency prevention programs, the results tended to explain the "one-sided emphasis [on] what needs to be done *to* and *by* the *offenders*." The sponsors of such programs rarely recognized that the youth or groups who were the focus of their efforts were only " responding to opportunities which the environment offers for the fulfillment of our common needs." [18] Accordingly, Robison looked for structural factors that made it more challenging for African American youth to achieve "recognition . . . adventure, and security" to establish why African American youth were more at risk for arrest early in their lives.[19]

In her essay, "How Effective are Current Juvenile Delinquency Preventive Programs?," Robison reported that in 1959 there were two main approaches to preventing or reducing juvenile delinquency. The first held the individual or family responsible for controlling behavior and relied on harsh forms of punishment in the belief that it was possible to beat deviant behavior out of a person. Those supporting the second held the community partially responsible for controlling or preventing delinquency. Those advocating for the first position tended to favor restraints on mobility such as curfews and increasingly onerous forms of punishment, whereas those supporting the second offered counseling, community centers, and recreational programs as methods for engaging youth.[20] Robison found that poor evaluation design and methodologies prevented either approach from demonstrating that it had positive effects on reducing juvenile delinquency. Therefore, she called for more rigorous and sophisticated evaluation designs, "[more precise] articulation of aims, methods, and operational definitions," and carefully drawn boundaries around their treatment areas to allow for the measurement of results. Significant advances in the field depended on the willingness of researchers to share data especially from efforts that had failed, and Robison urged them to model their evaluation practices on those used in the "true experiments in the physical sciences."[21]

On these issues, the psychologist Kenneth B. Clark admitted that the disproportionately high incidence of delinquency among young African Americans was incontestable, noting that in 1957 alone, the police had arrested as many as eighty thousand African American youth between the ages of ten and seventeen years old for juvenile delinquency. In his

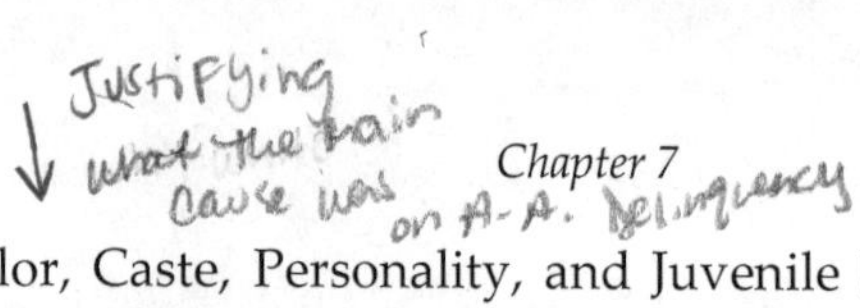

essay, "Color, Caste, Personality, and Juvenile Delinquency," Clark examined two studies whose samples were too small for generalizing but afforded him an opportunity to explore aspects of juvenile delinquency that had often been overlooked. For example, acts of delinquency involving white youth attacking African Americans or property owned by African Americans in neighborhoods undergoing desegregation, places that Clark described as "tension areas."[22] In such communities, Clark pointed to the influence of white elders who supported racially based acts of violence because they believed in segregation, despite affirming principles such as fair play, equality, and non-discrimination.[23] Clark believed that when white youth committed racist acts they "[rejected] moral considerations as having any actual validity [and thought that they might] indeed develop a tough, cynical, might is right, 'realistic' approach to life which they interpret as more 'honest' than the hypocrisy of their elders."[24]

Another form of delinquency that often escaped police action because it was almost exclusively associated with affluent, white suburban children, whom Clark termed "privileged delinquents," comprised behaviors that now might be classified as bullying. These perpetrators also expressed the moral flaws of a social order that accorded them high levels of privilege and unearned status, as Clark explained:[25]

> the essence of privileged delinquency includes patterns of social cruelty. Instead of overt, anti-social gangs, there are tight cliques which assert and reinforce their in-group status by exclusion and ruthless compulsion toward conformity. . . . If delinquency is to be defined in terms of its essentials of lack of social sensitivity, lack of empathy, a callous disregard for the humanity and dignity of others, a punitive and seductive approach to others who are considered weak and defenseless, then these privileged individuals must be considered delinquent despite the fact that they are not part of the court records and the presently available delinquency statistics.[26]

Aware that the child-rearing practices of middle-class African Americans differed in that they stressed "respectability," which involved behaving carefully in public and avoiding or removing themselves from social situations that seemed likely to lead to conflicts with the police, Clark concluded that middle-class African American youth were expending a great deal of psychic energy in everyday life. Further, he felt that the psychological damage that middle-class African American youth suffered while donning the mask of deference and respectability required by their elders prompted them to behave contemptuously toward working class or low-income African Americans:

> Children from middle and upper class Negro groups tend to react to their racial frustrations and conflicts by withdrawn and submissive behavior in contrast to the overt, aggressive patterns of lower-class

> Negro children. . . . The middle and upper class Negro groups may have a lower incidence of delinquency in their children but may be required to pay for it by a higher frequency of self-hatred, internal conflicts, emotional disturbance, and confusion about self and his group.[27]

The sociologist Hylan Lewis offered a critical evaluation of *Juvenile Delinquency among Negroes in the United States*, describing it as: "a kind of clinical showcase" whose main purpose was "a clearer understanding of the complex relationship between the psychology of minority status and the concretes of antisocial behavior."[28] Lewis recognized the challenges faced by Thompson in "[assembling] papers that will together supply comprehensive coverage, coherence, and discrimination to this subject,"[29] but he found that the 1959 Yearbook was marred by too much duplication, too many dated materials, and too many gaps in coverage. Lewis thought that many of the conjectures reported in the Yearbook required "rigid testing" to determine their current "cogency," and that the authors had failed to explain "why some [youth] become delinquent [and others who were similarly situated did] not."[30] Neither did they account for the rapid rise of delinquency among affluent, suburban-dwelling, white youth nor how much weight should "minority status," "class status," or "self-conceptions" receive when explaining the high incidence of delinquency among African American youth.[31] For Lewis, the 1959 Yearbook had contributed to the contemporaneous understanding of delinquency, and he commended criminologist Joseph D. Lohman for pointing out the significant role that the police played in the arrest and labeling of delinquents when he observed that the increase in delinquency reflected essentially an increase in the negative interactions between youth and the police. Lewis further commended the Yearbook's authors for their refusal to "adopt a position of futility with respect to the problems related to understanding juvenile delinquency" and for openly discussing the problems they encountered in developing theory and research while simultaneously attempting to apply that theory and research.[32]

Several months later, on September 9, 1959, the US Commission on Civil Rights issued the *Report of the United States Commission on Civil Rights, 1959*, on the second anniversary of the Civil Rights Act of 1957. Much like the Fair Employment Practices Committee that had preceded it by nearly two decades, the US Commission on Civil Rights had a purely investigatory and advisory role authorizing it to "investigate, to study, to appraise, and to make findings and recommendations . . . [but] . . . *not* to be a Commission for the enforcement of civil rights."[33] In his autumn 1959 editorial, "Civil Rights in the United States," Thompson described this *Report* as making "some important recommendations calculated to ameliorate many untoward conditions which were discovered." Accordingly, he encouraged his readers to "take the first opportunity to read the *Report*" and promised to give it fuller, critical coverage in one of the *Journal*'s subsequent issues.[34] With those words of introduction, Thompson reprinted "Part Five, Conclusion: The Problem as a Whole" from the *Report*.

In the autumn of 1959, not only was Dwight Eisenhower in the last year of his presidency, but Howard University's president had also begun his final year in office. When he reached the mandatory retirement age of sixty-five on June 30, 1955, the Board of Trustees retired Mordecai Wyatt Johnson but immediately reappointed him as "President of Howard University for . . . five (5) years beginning July 1, 1955, and expiring June 30, 1960."[35] Thus, Johnson's presidency would end in ten months as would his thirty-four-year sponsorship of Thompson's work on policy research and civil rights.

NOTES

1. Charles H. Thompson, "Editorial Comment: With All Deliberate Speed," *The Journal of Negro Education*, 27, no. 4 (Autumn 1958): 437.
2. Ibid., 438.
3. Charles H. Thompson, "Editorial Comment: The Moral Issue in Desegregation," *The Journal of Negro Education*, 28, no. 1 (Winter 1959): 1.
4. "Discrimination and the Christian Conscience," *The Journal of Negro Education*, 28, no. 1 (Winter 1959): 69.
5. Charles H. Thompson, "The Moral Issue in Desegregation," 2; "Discrimination and the Christian Conscience," 68.
6. Charles H. Thompson, "Editorial Comment: Mr. Huntley's Astounding Proposal," *The Journal of Negro Education*, 28, no. 2 (Spring 1959): 85–86.
7. Ibid., 87.
8. Ibid., 90–91.
9. Ibid., 88–89.
10. Ibid., 90.
11. Ibid.
12. Ibid., 90–91.
13. Charles H. Thompson, "Editorial Comment: Juvenile Delinquency among Negroes in the United States," *The Journal of Negro Education*, 28, no. 3 (Summer 1959): 187.
14. Joseph D. Lohman, "Juvenile Delinquency: A Social Dimension," *The Journal of Negro Education*, 28, no. 3 (Summer 1959): 294.
15. Thompson, "Juvenile Delinquency among Negroes in the United States," 187–88.
16. Ibid., 188.
17. Miriam Dinerman, "Sophia Moses Robison." In *Jewish Women: A Comprehensive Historical Encyclopedia*. March 1, 2009. Jewish Women's Archive, accessed August 15, 2017, https://jwa.org/encyclopedia/article/robison-sophia-moses.
18. Sophia M. Robison, "How Effective are Current Juvenile Delinquency Programs," *The Journal of Negro Education*, 28, no. 3 (Summer 1959): 351.
19. Ibid., 364.
20. Ibid., 352.
21. Ibid., 365.

22. Kenneth B. Clark, "Color, Class, Personality, and Juvenile Delinquency," *The Journal of Negro Education*, 28, no. 3 (Summer 1959): 248.
23. Ibid., 248–49.
24. Ibid., 249.
25. Ibid.
26. Ibid., 250.
27. Ibid., 248.
28. Hylan Lewis, "Juvenile Delinquency among Negroes—A Critical Summary," *The Journal of Negro Education*, 28, no. 3 (Summer 1959): 371.
29. Ibid., 372.
30. Ibid., 373.
31. Ibid.
32. Ibid., 387.
33. US Commission on Civil Rights, *Report of the United States Commission on Civil Rights* (Washington, DC: US Government Printing Office, 1959), x.
34. Charles H. Thompson, "Editorial Comment: Civil Rights in the United States," *The Journal of Negro Education*, 28, no. 4 (Autumn 1959): 389.
35. Logan, *Howard University: The First Hundred Years, 1867–1967*, 444.

In this chapter, the courts were still slow moving to desegregate schools, mob violence was also an issue in response to Little Rock. Instead of criticizing the courts on their slow moving decision to desegregate, Thompson decides to do the opposite and praise them. we also see churches were in favor and supporting desegregation, but at the same time another controversy arose from a newscaster at NBC that told African Americans to stop relying on the court's decision to desegregate

There was also discussion among youth delinquency and the role African American youths played in response to white children bullying African American children to that.

EIGHT

Reassessing Civil Rights Goals

The 1960s

The midpoint of Mordecai Wyatt Johnson's final year as president of Howard University found Thompson in a reflective mood. He still believed that the modern African American struggle for civil rights had hinged upon "the policy decision . . . to make a frontal attack upon segregation in all phases of the Negro's life,"[1] and he attributed the decision to attack segregation as inherently discriminatory as much to "grassroots pressure [as to] the deliberate decision of the NAACP."[2] Thompson was approaching Howard University's mandatory retirement age of sixty-five, and whether the tributaries of his reflections had their source in recent history or in his personal experience, Thompson strove to identify civil rights goals then worth pursuing.

Significant among these were landmark higher education cases for which he served as an expert witness for the National Association for the Advancement of Colored People (NAACP) Legal Defense and Educational Fund, Inc. In his winter 1960 editorial, "Some Unfinished Business for the 1960s," Thompson specifically noted two of those cases, *Sweatt v. Painter* (1950) and *McLaurin v. Oklahoma* (1950) that subsequently had inspired litigation in Delaware, Kentucky, Louisiana, and Maryland that resulted in the admission by December 1951 of "several hundred Negro students [into] formerly all-white publicly-supported universities in seven states."[3] Another case, *District of Columbia v. John R. Thompson Co., Inc.* (1952), was close to his heart because of the involvement of his wife, Mae Stewart Thompson, Charles Hamilton Houston, Mary Church Terrell, and others in picketing and supporting the litigation that opened restaurants in the nation's capital and catalyzed the successful movement to desegregate Washington, DC. Similar cases concerned with desegregation were *Morgan v. Virginia* (1946), and *Keys v. Carolina Coach Company* (1955), and *NAACP v. St. Louis-San Francisco Railway Com*pany (1955) that had opened up transportation on railroad trains and buses that traveled across state lines, ending "one of the most disgraceful exhibitions of intolerance and intransigence that [the nation] had witnessed since Reconstruction."[4] Other interests of Thompson were events that he had rarely mentioned in his editorials. He recalled the murder and lynching of fourteen-year-old Emmett Till and the shooting of Gus Courts for registering African Americans to vote. He noted the assassination of the Reverend George Lee to curtail his voter registration activities, which had all occurred in 1955 in Thompson's native state of Mississippi, as well as the attack by Southern white collegians that had caused Autherine Lucy to flee the University of Alabama. Then in 1956, the combined efforts of the legislatures in Alabama, Florida, Georgia, Texas, South Carolina, and Virginia had sought to put the NAACP out of business by financially ruining the organization. Virginia had adopted legislation permitting the state to control any public school that had been ordered by a court to desegregate, and some Northern newspapers and citizens sought to appease Southern whites by advising the NAACP to "Go slow, now" in advancing school desegregation there. These various events and the successes of the Montgomery Bus Boycott and the efforts of African Americans in Tuskegee, Alabama, to exercise their right to vote reinforced Thompson's conviction that:

> America cannot leave the according on even the most simple and elemental rights of Negroes in the South solely or even primarily to the consciences of most Southern whites. Almost without exception every advance has come because of legal prodding, often coercion. [In fact, the push to] "turn the clock back" [placed America] only a little in advance of the Union of South Africa [in December 1959].[5]

Nonetheless, Thompson had detected a willingness on the part of "a growing minority of Southern whites . . . to stand up and be counted on the side of moral right and legal justice."[6] While recognizing that the support of allies was essential, Thompson renewed his calls for African Americans to demonstrate self-determination, leadership, and financial support for the organizations that were committed to these ends:

> if Negroes are going to obtain their rights as first-class American citizens, they will have to fight for them; and primarily under their own leadership. Many whites, North and South, have helped and will continue to help in this struggle, but Negroes themselves will have to bear the major share of leadership.[7]

As was intimated previously with reference to South Africans, by 1960, the degree to which African Americans enjoyed equal citizenship rights often served as a litmus test of the United States' intentions toward the newly independent nations in Asia and Africa in the superpower competition between the Soviet Union and the United States. Thompson held that African Americans had a responsibility to oppose violations of human rights wherever they occurred.

At this point, Thompson outlined six objectives for advancing African American civil rights on a comprehensive scale: strengthening the Civil Rights Act of 1957, adding three million new African American voters in the South, defeating the use of pupil assignment plans and other ploys to evade desegregation, fully desegregating public facilities, fighting against housing discrimination and discriminatory lending practices, and undertaking the educational campaigns and programs that were capable of undoing the psychological damage stemming from racial segregation.

Thompson's spring 1960 editorial, "Desegregation Pushed off Dead Center," reported that "On February 1, 1960, a handful of Negro students from North Carolina A & T College in Greensboro, NC, started a brush fire which in the brief period of two months has assumed the proportions of an unquenchable conflagration."[8]

For his readers who were unfamiliar with the issues involved, Thompson provided a brief primer on the practice that had come under siege:

> In most of the larger stores in the South, as well as in the rest of the country for that matter, lunch counters are maintained for the convenience of their patrons. In the South, the practice or custom has developed where white patrons of the lunch counters—where seating is available—can sit down and be served; and Negroes, if they wish to be served, have to eat while standing, or have their food served in containers to be taken out, or not served at all, or in a few instances be required to occupy either a separate counter or a segregated section of the general counter. Tired of this humiliating practice, four students went to a variety store in Greensboro, quietly seated themselves at the lunch counter reserved for whites and courteously requested service. They were refused; but they continued to sit at the counter until the store closed for the day. The next day they were joined by a larger number of students, with much the same results. This simple demonstration caught the imagination of Negro college students throughout the South, at first in North Carolina, and spread quickly to other states, so that at present such demonstrations have occurred in scores of cities in all Southern states except Mississippi. Moreover, sympathy demonstrations have taken place in many Northern communities, and in a few instances white college students in the South, as well as the North, have joined the protest movement in one way or another.[9]

Thompson described in some detail the philosophy of nonviolence that had inspired the students and outlined their protocol for avoiding physical or verbal confrontations with store managers or patrons. He pointed out that the store managers had reacted initially by closing the lunch counters rather than serve the students, but they eventually called the police and had upwards of one thousand students arrested on "charges of trespassing, disorderly conduct," or similar charges.[10] Refusing to limit their protest to private stores, the students also conducted sit-in campaigns at "lunch counters in publicly-owned facilities, such as courthouses and city hall, and city libraries and quasi-public facilities such as those in bus stations and railroad terminals."[11] Surprisingly, the police often had conducted themselves with restraint, and yet there were episodes involving "[the] usual unnecessary brutality."[12] One of the worst episodes occurred when the mayor ordered firefighters in Orangeburg, South Carolina, to turn their hoses on the students during freezing temperatures. As a result, the water struck the students with such force that it peeled the skin from several students' faces, a measure of brutality that Thompson likened to police attacks on unarmed demonstrators in South Africa.[13]

There were strong moral justifications and solid legal grounds for the students' protest, but he also realized that "it is going to take intelligence, time, money, and patience before we can expect a definitive decision from the highest tribunal."[14] Thompson believed that if the students had discussed their plan of action even with the high command of the NAACP, they would have been advised against proceeding—on the assumption that it would be unwise to precipitate many different legal cases in different localities simultaneously. Nonetheless, Thompson opined that the students had developed "the better strategy."[15] By the spring of 1960, however, Thompson disagreed with the students' plans to let the police arrest them in such numbers that they would fill the jails to overflowing. He was concerned that they were unnecessarily risking physical and mental injury or worse by subjecting themselves to imprisonment in the South, and he also noted the consequences of their having a police record for their prospects for future employment, especially in the cases of students who planned to pursue teaching careers. Those concerns notwithstanding, Thompson thought that the students' protest was:

> a blessing in disguise [that] . . . has pushed the desegregation struggle off "dead center" where it seems to have been resting for the past two or three years. We have been winning court battles but apparently losing the propaganda war. The "sit-down" campaign has revitalized our struggle at a time when it was needed most, and has given us the initiative in this propaganda war.[16]

Thompson also was favorably impressed by the "extent to which this 'sit-down' campaign has fired the imagination of otherwise lukewarm or apathetic white students in the North, and motivated white students in the South to assist the Negro students in their campaign," succeeding in[17]
:

> [galvanizing] and [unifying] Negro communities all over the country to an extent hardly equaled before. Most of those who would have advised against such a campaign before it was started have since become ardent converts and supporters. Even the President of the United States, who has never given the leadership which one should expect of the Chief Executive, even in court-ordered desegregation, had been stimulated to give some aid and comfort to the oppressed, even though equivocal.[18]

Thompson further felt that having made a breakthrough in the struggle for public support, African Americans had to maintain their sense of perspective: segregationists were not through fighting to uphold white supremacy, and victory would not come to the supporters of desegregation overnight. On the contrary, there would be frustrating losses and disappointments in the days ahead, and he, therefore, encouraged his readers to steel themselves against adversity while still maintaining confidence and faith in the ultimate success of their mission. He concluded the editorial, "Desegregation Pushed off Dead Center," by warning "we must not fool ourselves. We know that this is just the beginning. This particular 'sit-down' campaign is both therapeutic and symbolic. Negroes will continue, I hope, to keep up the pressure until every vestige of second-class treatment has been abolished."[19]

Spring 1960 struck Thompson as an opportune time for deciding whether the sit-in movement fit into "a more comprehensive and articulate statement of [the civil rights movement's] objectives and strategy."[20] Therefore, he encouraged the leaders of the National Urban League and the NAACP to "exchange . . . views [with] our grassroots leadership," including the Reverend Dr. Martin Luther King, Jr., and the leaders of the Southern Christian Leadership Council. To illustrate the kind of conversation that he had in mind, Thompson pointed to the "by-invitation-only" meeting of sixty-two lawyers that had been sponsored by the NAACP in Washington, DC, between March 18 and 20, 1960. Ostensibly, the meeting was to organize support for those students whom the police had arrested for participating in the sit-ins. Nonetheless, the conferees used the opportunity to develop an overall strategy for capitalizing on the momentum generated by the sit-ins.[21] In this meeting, attended by Thurgood Marshall and James M. Nabrit, Jr., the NAACP had set aside forty thousand dollars for the students' legal defense, as reported in the Washington edition of the *Afro American*. This development led Thompson to hope that the leaders of the various branches of the movement would begin a conversation that would fashion a mutually agreeable strategy for sustaining their campaign for civil rights.[22]

As early as 1932, Thompson's mentor, Dwight Oliver Wendell Holmes, had urged the leaders of African American higher education institutions to limit unhealthy duplication of campuses and the resulting competition. Holmes championed "scientific studies; . . . cooperative action among the colleges; and . . . plans [for] . . . building up adequate endowments in order to insure a stable income for each institution in carrying forward the program assigned to it" to save many of the nation's historically black colleges and universities from ruin.[23] Subsequent surveys, including the *National Survey of the Higher Education of Negroes* (1942), had confirmed Holmes' recommendations as had Thompson's 1958 Yearbook, but Holmes' agenda had received little attention. By 1961, the problem had assumed the dimensions of an impending catastrophe, with 43 percent of African American colleges at risk of losing regional accreditation.

There were a few bright spots in this gloomy picture: the leaders of Spelman College, Morehouse College, and Atlanta University had forged partnerships that transformed their campuses into magnets for the best and brightest African American youth. Allen University and Benedict College also had developed creative partnerships that Frederick D. Patterson, the president of the Phelps-Stokes Fund, described as permitting the faculty at Benedict College to teach courses in physics and mathematics for both colleges, whereas the teachers at Allen University provided instruction in home economics and business.[24] In addition, the consolidation of Dillard University and Huston-Tillotson College had not only bolstered their competitiveness but also had won additional support from private philanthropic foundations such as the General Education Board and the Rosenwald Fund.[25] Accordingly, Thompson felt that it would be possible to salvage 80 percent of African American private colleges with "more money, more effective organization of [their programs], and better utilization of present resources."[26] In a letter to Horace Mann Bond dated November 28, 1959, Thompson outlined the 1960 issue of the Yearbook, *The Negro Private and Church-related College,* as a means to achieve this.[27] The issue had twenty-three chapters divided into four parts. Section one provided information on the origin and development, contemporaneous status, and educational significance of the sixty African American private and church-related colleges in the South. Section two was outstanding in that it included essays from the leaders of twelve of the thirteen religious denominations that funded one or more African American college in 1960, explicitly stating the policy guiding their respective denominations' involvement in African American higher education. The focus of section three of the Yearbook was strengthening the various colleges' financial positions and competitiveness; section four provided two critical evaluations of the Yearbook from the perspective of a leader of a denominational board of education and a longtime policymaker in Afro America who was then a consultant to the Ford Foundation.

According to Thompson, the average African American private college in the South in 1960 was "a relatively small institution—too small, in fact, to operate economically and effectively as an autonomous educational unit,"[28] which to survive required increased enrollment or a merger with another college. Because nineteen African American private or church-related colleges were located in the same city, and nearly three-fourths of them were not fully accredited, Thompson found merger to be the most credible solution. Because the African American private and church-related colleges paid the lowest faculty salaries, they did not attract talented faculty. The missionary spirit that had motivated Thompson and the other top scholars of his generation to enter college teaching had vanished and these small African American private and church-related colleges had not kept "pace either with the cost of living or salaries paid by government and industry."[29] To raise faculty salaries, Thompson predicted that they would need "to raise [the] salary floor for all ranks by at least $500 over [the] 1959–60 [amounts], and in many critical fields [they would] have to go as high as $1,000."[30] If for the foreseeable future "Negro colleges will have to rely largely upon Negro teachers both because of the tight market and racial considerations," the relatively low numbers of African Americans who were pursuing studies leading to the doctorate would be insufficient, and he felt that reversing this trend was crucial to the survival of African American higher education.[31]

On the other hand, the growth of African American public colleges in the South that could be traced to the *Gaines* (1938) decision whereby the Supreme Court required the segregated states to provide substantially equal higher educational opportunities to African American citizens within their states, had added graduate and professional programs including law schools and medical schools. By 1960, these African American public colleges in the South had "better plants, more equipment, higher paid teachers and generally lower student costs" than African American private colleges in the South, leaving the private African American colleges to fill the gaps in order to be educationally relevant.[32]

In his essay, "The Negro Church-Related College: A Critical Summary," Robert C. Weaver stated that too many of the contributors to the 1960 Yearbook had underestimated human factors in making their recommendations. Weaver felt that although "rapid mergers and even more immediate abandonment" were fine as far as logical solutions went, those proposals had failed to recognize "the very pride in affiliation which made the institutions possible in the first place."[33] The contributors who perceived accreditation as a "corrective force" were equally mistaken; although useful in identifying those colleges that were likely to fail, this mechanical device had less value when "[identifying] the colleges and junior colleges which merit support."[34] An economist and expert in labor studies, Weaver felt that accreditation criteria were inappropriate for solving "human problems" such as the restructuring of African American private higher education in the South.[35] To validate his point, Weaver recalled conducting site visits at merged colleges where the denominations involved had equal numbers of seats on the board of directors, and that one year later, he had returned to those campuses to find that serious internal divisions had blocked most, if not all, progress toward the creation of stronger, more sustainable institutions. In contrast, he had also completed inspections at "five other church-related Negro colleges where newly selected presidents [were] making significant progress in upgrading the standards and performance of their schools." For Weaver, the inescapable conclusion was that "Men and women are more important than machinery—a fact that received insufficient recognition in most of the . . . chapters [in the 1960 Yearbook]."[36]

Like William J. Trent, Jr., executive director of the United Negro College Fund, Weaver felt the future of African American private higher education hinged on a "policy decision to stay relatively small with [substantial] resources" to fulfill their colleges' missions. Or they could let weak finances make this choice for them.[37] On the other hand, Weaver noted, "the good Negro church-related college" has a "vital place" in higher education in the South. By placing greater emphasis "[on developing] men and women who [can] think, express themselves well, and feel at home with new ideas and complex issues," these colleges would be of real value to the South and the nation.[38] Taking a similar position to that articulated in 1958 by Martin D. Jenkins, Weaver suggested, "the private Negro college can and should accelerate racial integration below the Mason and Dixon line."[39] The sit-in movement had recently shifted attention toward these colleges' "historic role" in fostering civil rights and the respect for human dignity as "dramatized by the activities of their students, the courageous stand of many trustees, presidents and faculties, and the public posture of the United Negro College Fund incident to the sit-ins."[40] The church-related colleges thus had between African Americans and whites the opportunity to close the gap between precept and deed by encouraging mergers within the various denominations that could give rise to "fewer and better colleges" that would prove to be a boon not only to the denominations, but to the South as well.[41] Weaver thought that in the long run:

> emphasis upon excellence is the only honest approach to the youth of our nation; but excellence is currently expensive, and if it is to be achieved and the rich tradition of the past is to be continued, the denominations must supply greater financial support to the colleges and junior colleges they so proudly sponsor. With this support, additional public acceptance and financial contributions, and able educational leadership, the church-related institutions can become a contemporary expression of the tribute paid to the better Negro private colleges by DuBois, [James Weldon] Johnson, and scores of others who found inspiration, learning, and ideals in these schools.[42]

NOTES

1. Charles H. Thompson, "Editorial Comment: Some Unfinished Business for the 1960s," *The Journal of Negro Education*, 29, no. 1 (Winter 1960): 1.
2. Ibid., 2.
3. Ibid., 1.
4. Ibid., 2.
5. Ibid., 4.
6. Ibid.
7. Ibid., 4–5.
8. Charles H. Thompson, "Editorial Comment: Desegregation Pushed off Dead Center," *The Journal of Negro Education*, 29, no. 2 (Spring 1960): 107.
9. Ibid., 107.
10. Ibid. 108.
11. Ibid.
12. Ibid.
13. Ibid.
14. Ibid., 109.
15. Ibid., 108, 110.
16. Ibid., 111.
17. Ibid.
18. Ibid.
19. Ibid.
20. Ibid.
21. "Lawyers to Confer on Sit-Down Tactics," *Afro American* (Washington, DC), March 15, 1960, accessed August 19, 2017, https://news.google.com/newspapers/p/afro?nid=BeIT3YV5QzEC&dat=19600315&printsec=frontpage&hl=en.
22. Ibid.; Thompson, "Desegregation Pushed Off Dead Center," 111.
23. Horace Mann Bond, "The Origin and Development of the Negro Church-Related College," *The Journal of Negro Education*, 29, no. 3 (Summer 1960): 225.
24. Frederick D. Patterson, "Duplication of Facilities and Resources of Negro Church-Related Colleges," *The Journal of Negro Education*, 29, no. 3 (Summer 1960): 370.
25. Ibid., 371.
26. Charles H. Thompson, "The Present Status of the Negro Private and Church-Related College," *The Journal of Negro Education*, 29, no. 3 (Summer 1960): 244.
27. Charles H. Thompson, letter to Horace Mann Bond, November 18, 1959, School of Education Papers, Moorland-Spingarn Research Center, Howard University Archives, Howard University, Box 1894, *Journal of Negro Education*.
28. Thompson, "The Present Status of the Negro Private and Church-Related College," 242–43.
29. Ibid., 243.
30. Ibid.
31. Ibid., 242.
32. Robert C. Weaver, "The Negro Private and Church-Related College: A Critical Summary," *The Journal of Negro Education*, 29, no. 3 (Summer 1960): 396.
33. Ibid., 396.
34. Ibid., 398.
35. Ibid., 396.
36. Ibid. 397.
37. Ibid., 398.
38. Ibid., 399.
39. Ibid.
40. Ibid.
41. Ibid.
42. Ibid., 400.

In this Chapter, Ray discusses Thompson reflecting on the various movements that had taken place, specifically the sit ins, and the attacks made to African Americans. While he understood the reasons behind students wanting Police to arrest them, he strongly disagreed because it would be on their record.

Thompson also reflected on higher education for African Americans. These buildings needed to receive adequate endowments in order to keep their doors open. Various colleges turned their campuses into opportunities for African Americans where they can receive the best college education. Here we also see there's an issue because of the low numbers of African Americans receiving a college education because of the tight market and racial concerns. However, Black colleges needed African American educators.

NINE

Inequality Persists and Takes New Forms

Rayford Logan had described the presidency of Mordecai Wyatt Johnson as the golden years of Howard University, and on April 20, 1960, Thompson traveled to New York City to discuss his ideas for the university's future with several members of the Howard University Board of Trustees. In an undated, single-page, single-spaced, typed document, "What do the Trustees Want? Another Mordecai? (Need Two Men)," Thompson recorded his thinking regarding the most pressing tasks facing Howard University and thought that a comprehensive survey of instruction at Howard University along the lines of the surveys described in the 1958 and 1960 issues of the Yearbook was necessary. According to Thompson:

> The most pressing problem at the University as a whole is the improvement of instruction in all of the schools and colleges. I am so convinced of this that, . . . I would recommend [to the new president] that a detailed survey be made of instruction in all the units of the University. And, I would involve all the members of the [teaching staff] in this survey because I would want the people who are responsible for instruction to know what the problems were firsthand, so that they would be in a better position to do something about them.[1]

In his autumn 1960 editorial, "Howard University Changes Leadership," Thompson noted Johnson's retirement and its significance and welcomed the incoming president James Madison Nabrit, Jr., and a new era in the university's history. In the editorial, Thompson's concern focused on the university, to which he had devoted his professional life, and evaluated its prospects for survival in an increasingly competitive and desegregated US higher education sector, measuring the progress that had been made toward its goal of becoming a first-class university during Johnson's years in office. He began this assessment by noting several milestones that had been a result of Mordecai Johnson's service as the first African American president and one who had served in that "capacity longer than any other president of Howard University."[2]

Thompson noted that having made his mark in the ministry, Johnson was a relative newcomer to African American higher education when he had accepted election as president of Howard University in 1926. Notwithstanding this, Johnson had proved to be a charismatic leader who fulfilled his duties in a thoughtful and highly disciplined fashion. Early in his tenure, Johnson had commissioned an external survey "of the needs and prospects of Howard University" and used this evidence to conclude that in a segregated society, "the Federal government had a moral obligation to the Negro minority which could be met only by the development of the University into a first-class institution." Believing that "Howard University should be made in fact, as well as in name, the 'Capstone of Negro Education,'" Johnson was "unusually successful in selling his program for Howard University to the Federal government," according to Thompson, for several influential members of Congress responded favorably to his proposals and budget requests. Moreover, "in 1928, he persuaded Congress to legalize its appropriations to the University, and in 1929, [during the Hoover administration] he convinced the Department of the Interior . . . to agree upon a plan for making Howard University a first-class institution, and to recommend appropriations accordingly." Subsequently, Johnson forged productive relationships with the Roosevelt, Truman, and Eisenhower administrations that he sustained until his retirement.[3]

In recognition of Johnson's prodigious intellect and his skills in diplomacy and persuasion, the National Association for the Advancement of Colored People awarded him the Spingarn Medal, its highest honor, in 1929. The university had blossomed under Johnson's stewardship: he raised the funding necessary to add "badly-needed buildings," increased the salaries of the teaching and non-teaching staff, and put the university and "its colleges on something approximating a sound financial basis."[4] During Johnson's tenure, federal appropriations for the university's expenses had grown from $221,000 annually in 1926 to $4,617,000 in 1960, and the university's physical plant increased in value from $2,057,270 to thirty-eight million dollars. Thompson also credited Johnson with having completed "most of the foundational work necessary for building a first-class university," including doubling student enrollment as well as the university's visibility and reputation.[5]

In appreciating these tangible contributions that Johnson had made, he also noted his indebtedness to Johnson's spirited defense of academic integrity and scholarship: "Despite all the hysteria about communism and other controversial issues such as court cases against segregation, during the greater part of his tenure, Dr. Johnson insisted that academic freedom be maintained at the University. It was and still is."[6] He also pointed out that Johnson's political acumen and his commitment to human rights had made the civil rights advocacy practiced by Thompson, Charles Hamilton Houston, James Madison Nabrit, Jr., and others possible, and he suggested that Johnson write his memoirs in order to "make a highly significant contribution to education in general and Negro education in particular."[7]

The editorial also paid attention to Howard's new president, James Madison Nabrit, Jr., a scholar of considerable merit who had begun as an assistant professor of law in 1936. Subsequently, Nabrit had served as "assistant to the President, Secretary of the University, Director of Public Relations, Acting President, and Dean of the School of Law." Thompson thought in fall 1960 that Howard University was, however, most in need of someone "to do for instruction and research what President Johnson [had done] for the physical, organizational, and financial aspects of the University."[8] The university urgently needed a large number of new faculty members to reduce the teacher-to-student ratio to acceptable levels and to add breadth and depth to its curriculum so that students could receive solid undergraduate, graduate, and professional educations. Noting that "the teacher-scholars already on staff" needed encouragement and support to produce more publishable research, Thompson called for large, new investments in "research and scholarly activities" and for expansion of the library's holdings and staff until they could accommodate significantly higher levels of faculty and student research. To permit these, there was a need for more resources for scholarships and research grants-in-aid to "attract and hold more students of the highest caliber."[9]

Nabrit's early "speeches, news releases, and other communications" had made it "crystal clear" that the emphasis of his administration would be on improving the university's "instruction and research and scholarly activity," and he announced his intention to evaluate all budget requests based on their contribution to bolstering the university's productivity in these areas. Thompson wished "President Nabrit the greatest possible success" and concluded his fall 1960 editorial with the following pledge of support:

> It has already been made clear that all the members of the Howard University community—students, faculty and non-teaching members of the staff—stand ready to give [Nabrit] their highest cooperation and [unstinting] support in moving the University forward in this decisive period of its history. We hope that Congress, Alumni, and friends of the University will do no less.[10]

In this issue of the *Journal*, Thompson also published the text of "Howard University Looks to the Future," Nabrit's first formal presidential address to the university on September 15, 1960. In that speech, Nabrit described his plans to:

> engage in our own comprehensive self-examination. In this, we shall marshal all of the resources the University has. Our objective is not simply that of solving current problems, whatever they may be. Our goal is to make Howard University a really outstanding university on the basis of recognized value standards and educational criteria. In essence, what we are going to undertake is, first, to study ourselves; and second, on the basis of this study, to establish long-range plans. But before such study we must reflect on our basic educational philosophy and objectives. We need, too, a review of the particular objectives for each school and college. We need to arrive at a determination of the kinds of students that we want and their numbers. We need to be very thoughtful and deliberate with respect to our decisions in the matter of what we propose to teach our students.[11]

It later became clear in Rayford Logan's *Howard University: The First Hundred Years* that Nabrit had also decided on that date to choose Thompson to direct the first self-study in the history of the university.[12]

After the publication of the autumn 1960 editorial, Thompson's voice did not appear until the publication of his editorial "African Education South of the Sahara" in the summer of 1961. In his absence, Hurley H. Doddy, an associate professor of education at Howard and associate editor of the *Journal*, had written the editorials for the magazine's winter 1961 and spring 1961 issues. On March 2, 1961, the university's Board of Trustees appointed Thompson to direct the university's first self-study naming Stanton L. Wormley to serve as acting dean of the Graduate School in Thompson's absence.[13] Determined to fulfill his new responsibilities without relinquishing his editorship, and as early as October 5, 1960, he asked sociologist E. Franklin Frazier to comment on a ten-page proposal that he had prepared detailing the 1961 Yearbook.[14] On the contrary, Thompson gave the 1961 issue of the Yearbook such attention that it ranked among the finest that he had edited, and in historian Horace Mann Bond's opinion, *African Education South of the Sahara* was Thompson's best Yearbook. Bond's essay, "Some Major Educational Problems in Africa South of the Sahara: A Critical Summary," stated:

> The first and the last impression of this reviewer of the 1961 Yearbook is that no previous volume in the series excels the present one, in timeliness, scope, and value. The Editor deserves a special commendation for having brought together contributors whose material, and insights, have never before been assembled in one piece, and with such competence.[15]

Moreover, Bond noted that the statistical data reported in this Yearbook were then the most current in print.

Thompson pointed out that the problems facing the twenty or more countries that had recently gained their independence there included "the difficult and unfamiliar tasks of nation-building and the development of machinery and personnel for the management of their own affairs, with all the problems that these entail."[16] Moreover, because "nation-building and the development of a soundly-based state [was] the main task of newly-independent countries" in sub-Saharan Africa, he had exhorted the contributors to the 1961 Yearbook to undertake to offer recommendations regarding the "broad, major educational objectives" that would allow newly independent nations to reach that goal[17]:

> While most of the basic problems are common to all the countries, there are differences in degree of importance, due to geography, politics, economics, culture, education, and the like. Some of the countries are farther along the road to nationhood than others; some have greater tribal diversity, with accompanying differences in language, customs, and other characteristics; some have a greater number of European or white settlers--a fact which enormously complicates the task of nation-building; some have a larger supply of trained personnel; some have experienced a greater amount of industrialization and urbanization; some have been exposed to differing colonial philosophies which have resulted in varied effects upon the countries involved and upon the task of nation-building, and so on. Thus, a closer look at the problems as they obtain in individual areas will be desirable, in order to obtain a more comprehensive grasp of the picture as a whole.[18]

African Education South of the Sahara consisted of four sections. In the first section, several authors assessed the legacy of colonialism and the challenges that tribalism, language diversity, antagonism between the practitioners of Islam and Christianity, and opposition from white settlers, for example, posed to national unity. The second section focused on the status of education in the region, with several authors finding significant restrictions on Africans' access to education by the colonial governments of England, France, Belgium, Portugal, and the white settler–led governments of Southern Rhodesia and South Africa. For example, describing Portugal's philosophy for educating Africans in their colonies of Angola and Mozambique, James Duffy, professor of Spanish at Brandeis University, wrote:

> It is foolish to suppose that a colonial power is going to carry out an educational reform in Africa which it has not yet accomplished at home. Portugal is a poor country, and this poverty is as often intellectual as it is economic. There are not enough teachers for Africa, not enough money, not enough interest. But there is also a more important consideration, and that is the design of the Salazar regime to see to it that the African majority does not become any more politically conscious than is metropolitan Portugal's rural majority. Salazarian sociology envisages the formation of a devout, semi-literate, hard-working and conservative African population. For them *ensino de adaptagao* [a three-year elementary program with all instruction in Portuguese] is sufficient. The government is confident that it can indoctrinate with Portuguese values that handful of students which goes beyond the

> *ensino* program. For the mass, a general policy of psychological assimilation; for the few, an intensive cultural and political assimilation. This is the purpose of the educational program in Portuguese Africa.[19]

In the third section of the Yearbook, "African Education South of the Sahara—Some Problems of Implementation," Thompson presented analyses of the support available through agencies such as the United Nations, the US State Department, and the limitations on such support posed by many of these African nations' preference for neutrality in the Cold War. Conditioning the support from missionary societies in the United States was the need to ensure that national leaders did not perceive this work as "subversive or detrimental to the existing regime."[20] The fourth and concluding part, "Some Major Educational Problems: A Critical Summary," featured essays by Karl Bigelow, professor of education and executive officer of the Afro-Anglo-American Program at Teachers College, Columbia University, and Horace Mann Bond, dean of the School of Education at Atlanta University.

In the first section of the Yearbook, "Common Problems in the Task of Nation Building," political scientist L. Gray Cowan found that in nearly every country in sub-Saharan Africa "generations of colonial control" had failed to prepare the indigenous people for the complexities of self-government or dealing with international politics.[21] Moreover, the tendency to maintain the national boundaries established by the former colonial governments that had ignored longstanding tribal and linguistic affiliations fueled conflicts, and in many of the new states the emergence of a one-party system had propelled new leaders to prominence and provided them with the resources for advancing their agendas for independence. In his perceptive essay, Cowan attributed these developments as follows:

> Characteristically the most militant nationalist parties were tightly disciplined bodies, whose organization reached down from the urban centers to the rural villages and whose leadership was concentrated in the hands of the charismatic leader typified by Kwame Nkrumah or Sekou Toure. The program they presented to the voters was simple but comprehensive--self-government and independence in the shortest possible time. Under these circumstances, there was little room left for the emergence of an opposition party. [Accordingly,] the one-party system . . . appears to be based on the broad consent of the people of the new African states and shows little likelihood of disappearing in the coming decade.[22]

Cowan foresaw many of the severe problems that the leaders of the new nations in sub-Saharan Africa would experience, particularly the need to increase productivity through industrialization, to raise the standard of living for a broad cross-section of their populations through manufacturing. This solution would, in turn, initially require investment capital and skilled technicians from abroad and cause foreigners to reap many of the economic benefits that citizens and voters had come to expect. A consequence of failing to deliver rapidly and economically on these promises would alienate the citizens whose support was crucial to national security, prosperity, and political stability, and to make matters worse, Cowan anticipated a broad, continuing role for "the former metropolitan powers" that would involve loans, grants, technical assistance, and military aid to intrude in local and national affairs.[23] Moreover, even if Pan Africanism then was an attractive concept, Cowan believed that political realities and the desire to hold onto power would prevent Nkrumah and other African leaders from promoting this unifying goal as well as African socialism.[24]

Rupert Emerson's essay suggested that redrawing national borders would only invite unstoppable chaos because the African empires that predated colonialism had not done much to develop a common political identity among people whose primary "social-political identification [was] with their tribe and with their immediate locality rather than with any hypothetical nation or with the state which has taken over from the colonial regime."[25] Indeed, it seemed to him more accurate to think of the independence movements in sub-Saharan Africa as movements to overthrow racist overlords and seize control of the government to oppose "the status of inferiority which both slavery and colonialism imposed upon the African people."[26] Emerson also correctly foresaw the problems posed by corruption and despotism in many of the newly arising nations by "a group of insiders [bent] on clinging to power and office for personal profit and enjoyment rather than for the promotion of the public good."[27] The historian Jacob Ade Ajayi's contribution in this section, "The Place of African History and Culture in the Process of Nation-Building in Africa South of the Sahara," challenged Emerson's assertions by pointing to the existence of political entities in Africa that not only predated colonialism, but also that had fostered a national identity. Ajayi called for more "research and more understanding . . . to determine what aspects of the past will be most relevant and in what way" in decision-making in the newly independent states.[28]

In his essay, recently retired sociologist E. Franklin Frazier identified industrialization, urbanization, education, higher education, and the development of economic classes as factors that fostered political cohesion and the development of a national identity in Africa South of the Sahara. Concurring with Frazier's assessment, in his essay, "Some Major Educational Problems in Africa South of the Sahara: A Critical Summary," Horace Mann Bond noted:

> Emerson's emphasis upon the evils of 'tribalism' would be depressing, were they not relieved by Frazier's description of how urbanization and industrialization have gone far to break down the tribal structure,

especially in cities; and that new associations, based on educational and social level, and occupation, have already in numerous places helped greatly to dissolve the old "tribal" strength.[29]

On the other hand, Thomas M. Franck, an expert in international law, pointed out in the first section of the Yearbook the threats to democratic governance that large enclaves of white settlers had posed in the Union of South Africa and Rhodesia, by putting "down deep roots in parts of Africa, generally in the best soil."[30] Franck found that white expatriates who might be recruited to assist in nation building presented much less of a problem:

> the expatriate is hired to . . . train Africans who will succeed him and will work at wages adjusted to a more realistic skilled-unskilled ratio[;] the "white settler," anxious to remain in Africa but utterly unprepared to live *as an African*, has a vested interest in retaining his standard of living, his end of the wage gap, while hoping that unskilled wages will gradually rise to meet his own. This expectation has been unfulfilled in the last ten years as European wages have almost everywhere risen *faster* than African.[31]

Franck identified "European political predominance" as the primary factor for the pervasive educational and economic discrimination practiced against Africans on behalf of white settlers and their children; obtaining an education for Africans, as in the case of South Africans, was often a complicated, expensive, and unrewarding enterprise[32]:

> an African parent, despite far lower income, must pay approximately three times as much as a white parent to educate his child to junior certificate standard (the minimum recognized for most employment purposes). While the European child is entitled to free public education and pays £11 for books and stationery, the African must pay £8 for tuition (a month's wages for many workers) and £26 for books and stationery. Moreover, the operation of the six-year-old Bantu Education Act is now being felt in a general lowering of standards in African education. Since its inception, the number of students matriculating has steadily declined, and in 1960 totaled only 128, or 18 percent of the entrants, compared with 46 percent before the Act came into force.[33]

Franck characterized the education provided to white settlers' children as reinforcing racist thinking and behavior while promoting allegiance to white supremacy, noting that racial discrimination also provided a means for overcompensating white colonists who would have been considered incompetent if objective measures such as level of education, skills, or productivity were applied. To perpetuate this system and limit the development of a white lower class:

> these whites [are given] skilled jobs beyond their capacity. Their incompetence is a charge on the economy, but it is accepted by other whites rather with the resignation of the noble family which has

endowed a remote but respectably rural curacy for an embarrassingly simpleminded son.[34]

Franck also pointed out that despite the criticism directed against African tribalism, large white settler communities also practiced a variety of tribalism, in these ways.

In the second section of the Yearbook that assessed the availability, quality, and affordability of education in sub-Saharan Africa, Bernard Fall, an associate professor of government at Howard University, challenged the position that Belgium had educated few Africans in its former colony, the Congo. According to Fall, the Congo's literacy rate of 50 percent was the highest in all of sub-Saharan Africa in 1960 with the education of girls being one of its significant accomplishments.[35] Moreover, the annual education budget of thirty-eight million dollars represented 15 percent of the colony's operating expenses. A result of this policy was that 65 percent of Congolese youth had received a primary education free of charge, which Fall contended to be "unmatched by any other country in Africa except Ghana."[36] Moreover, Fall thought that vocational education in the Congo had no rivals in all of Africa.[37] Notwithstanding these strengths, Belgium had made two fatal mistakes that contributed to regional instability: its colonial administrators had failed to prepare "a responsible political elite" and denied potential leaders the practical experience that might have prepared them to govern. The admission requirements for high schools were so high that few went beyond elementary school, and indeed, the majority of the Congolese never acquired a university education.[38]

It mattered little whether one examined education in established nations such as Liberia and Ethiopia, newly independent ones like Ghana, Nigeria, and Sierra Leone, or oppressive, racially segregated countries such as Rhodesia and South Africa; one reached the same conclusion: few school systems prepared Africans for high school or beyond. As a result, many of the leaders of the new African nations came from the ranks of teachers, one of the few professional occupations to which an educated African could aspire.[39] Therefore, teacher training held the key to not only expanding public education in sub-Saharan Africa but also reducing these nations' reliance on educated expatriates.

Accordingly, Raymond J. Smyke had identified several affordable options for expanding teacher training. In his essay, "Problems of Teacher Supply and Demand in Africa South of the Sahara," Smyke proposed the creation of several "regional [teacher-training] centers, one for English and one for French-speaking Africa" capable of preparing as many as five hundred teachers simultaneously.[40] He also urged the adoption of teacher-training correspondence courses such as those pioneered in Indonesia to reduce the current and projected shortages in primary, secondary, and vocational education teachers.[41] Horace Mann Bond, then dean of the

School of Education at Atlanta University, sounded a note of caution in his essay, "Some Major Educational Problems in Africa South of the Sahara: A Critical Summary." Bond doubted whether any of the states examined in the 1961 Yearbook could afford to spend more than ten or twenty dollars per person for all governmental services. He also was leery whether the leaders of these new nations would make the same sacrifices as China and the Soviet Union had when expanding free public education to their citizens.[42] The educational, economic, and political challenges facing African leaders were "immense"; nonetheless, Bond realized that the expansion of public education in sub-Saharan Africa also represented "a great human opportunity." He concluded his essay with the hope that despite its disappointing performance to date, the United States would provide more aid for African education and development for moral reasons as well as the geopolitical advantages made possible from allying with these nations.[43]

Thompson wrote his fall 1961 editorial, "The Need for more 'Deliberate Speed' in School Desegregation," in response to the publication of *Education: 1961 US Commission on Civil Rights Report, Book 2*. This commission found that even the slow pace of school desegregation between 1954 and 1959 had slowed to a halt between 1960 and 1961, with only 7 percent of African American youth in the South attending public schools with Southern white students in 1961, and these mostly as a result of court orders. The situation had become so deplorable that the majority of the commissioners recommended the use of sanctions to hasten the pace of desegregation, and called on Congress to pass legislation that would authorize the US Attorney General to initiate lawsuits that would end the impasse over desegregation while imposing financial penalties on those states operating racially segregated public schools. For example, the commissioners thought that the amount of federal financial support that a state received should reflect the extent to which that state's school districts had desegregated. Furthermore, the commissioners urged the immediate end to federal financing for racially segregated public colleges and universities, and four of the six commissioners also thought that the policy of terminating federal grants should also apply to segregated private colleges and universities. The commissioners had discovered that many public libraries in the South that received funding under the Library Services Act of 1956 still practiced segregation or provided grossly inferior services to African Americans as compared with whites, and they called upon the Kennedy administration to terminate all the support that such segregated libraries were receiving from the federal government.

Thompson highlighted the recommendations in the *Report* that endorsed promising new federal programs that seemed capable of reducing the opportunity and achievement gaps that African Americans experienced as a result of decades of racially segregated public schooling. The commissioners urged the implementation of experimental programs piloted outside the South that had achieved promising results, for they demonstrated that African Americans' achievement was much higher with access to high-quality educational opportunities. Thompson underscored the findings of the *Report* that traced the transmission of the educational damages from segregation from one "generation of students to the next by teachers who were the victims of the same system." He urged the commissioners rather than making the funding for these programs available only to the states that colleges and universities should receive it under the National Defense Education Act to avoid it being "hampered by the indifference, inertia, antagonism, and archaic customs of many of the states which need the programs the most."[44] Aware of the likelihood that there would be a delay before Congress responded to the commission's recommendations, Thompson implored private philanthropic foundations to fund this program in the interim. With the publication of *Education: 1961 US Commission on Civil Rights Report, Book 2,* Thompson saw an opportunity to move beyond desegregation as the sole remedy for the discrimination experienced by African Americans in the dual system. In his fall 1961 editorial, Thompson endorsed a series of federal equal educational opportunities programs, such as the Federal TRIO Programs, that Congress subsequently would pass as part of President Lyndon Baines Johnson's War on Poverty.

NOTES

1. Charles H. Thompson, "What do the Trustees Want? Another Mordecai? (Need Two Men)," (n.d.), School of Education Papers, Moorland-Spingarn Research Center, Howard University Archives, Howard University, Box 1894, *Journal of Negro Education.*
2. Charles H. Thompson, "Editorial Comment: Howard University Changes Leadership," *The Journal of Negro Education,* 29, no. 4 (Autumn 1960): 409.
3. Ibid., 409.
4. Ibid., 409.
5. Ibid., 409–10.
6. Ibid. 410.
7. Ibid., 410.
8. Ibid.
9. Ibid., 411.
10. Ibid.
11. James M. Nabrit, Jr., "Howard University Looks to the Future," *The Journal of Negro Education,* 29, no. 4 (Autumn 1960): 417.
12. Logan, *Howard University: The First Hundred Years, 1867–1967,* 575.
13. Ibid., 463.
14. Charles H. Thompson, letter to E. Franklin Frazier, October 5, 1960, School of Education Papers, Moorland-Spingarn Research Center, Howard University Archives, Howard University, Box 1894, *Journal of Negro Education.*
15. Horace Mann Bond, "Some Major Educational Problems in Africa South of the Sahara: A Critical Summary," *The Journal of Negro Education,* 30, no. 3 (Summer 1961): 358.
16. Charles H. Thompson, "Editorial Comment: African Education South of the Sahara," *The Journal of Negro Education,* 30, no. 3 (Summer 1961): 173.

17. Ibid., 175.
18. Ibid., 173–74.
19. James Duffy, "Portuguese Africa (Angola and Mozambique): Some Crucial Problems and the Role of Education in Their Resolution," *The Journal of Negro Education*, 30, no. 3 (Summer 1961): 299, 301.
20. Frank T. Wilson, "The Future of Missionary Enterprise in Africa South of the Sahara," *The Journal of Negro Education*, 30, no. 3 (Summer 1961): 327.
21. L. Gray Cowan, "The Current Political Status and Significance of Africa South of the Sahara," *The Journal of Negro Education*, 30, no. 3 (Summer 1961): 180.
22. Ibid.
23. Ibid., 181.
24. Ibid., 181, 184–85.
25. Rupert Emerson, "Crucial Problems Involved in Nation-Building in Africa," *The Journal of Negro Education*, 30, no. 3 (Summer 1961): 195.
26. Ibid., 196.
27. Ibid., 202.
28. J. F. Ade Ajayi, "The Place of African History and Culture in the Process of Nation-Building in Africa South of the Sahara," *The Journal of Negro Education*, 30, no. 3 (Summer 1961): 213.
29. Horace Mann Bond, "Some Major Educational Problems in Africa South of the Sahara: A Critical Summary," *The Journal of Negro Education*, 30, no. 3 (Summer 1961): 359.
30. Thomas M. Franck, "European Communities in Africa," *The Journal of Negro Education*, 30, no. 3 (Summer 1961): 224. Thomas M. Franck had served as a consultant to the development of the constitutions adopted in the African nations of Tanzania, Zimbabwe, and Sierra Leone.
31. Ibid., 226.
32. In their essays in section two of the 1961 Yearbook, John H. Wheeler and Franklin Parker concurred with Franck's assessment about the negative role of white settlers in South Africa and Rhodesia. See John H. Wheeler, "Apartheid Implemented by Education in South Africa," *The Journal of Negro Education*, 30, no. 3 (Summer 1961): 241–50; and Franklin Parker, "Education in the Federation of Rhodesia and Nyssaland," *The Journal of Negro Education*, 30, no. 3 (Summer 1961): 286–93.
33. Franck, "European Communities in Africa," 226.
34. Ibid., 225.
35. Bernard B. Fall, "Education in the Republic of The Congo," *The Journal of Negro Education*, 30, no. 3 (Summer 1961): 267–68.
36. Ibid., 268.
37. Ibid., 270.
38. Ibid., 267, 270–72.
39. Raymond J. Smyke, "Problems of Teacher Supply and Demand in Africa South of the Sahara," *The Journal of Negro Education*, 30, no. 3 (Summer 1961): 338.
40. Ibid., 339.
41. Ibid., 338, 339, 341–42.
42. Horace Mann Bond, "Some Major Educational Problems in Africa South of the Sahara: A Critical Summary," 359.
43. Ibid., 364.
44. Charles H. Thompson, "Editorial Comment: The Need for More 'Deliberate Speed" in School Desegregation," *The Journal of Negro Education*, 30, no. 4 (Autumn 1961): 367.

TEN

Confirmation or Reset?

During the second year of the Kennedy administration in a neighborhood about three miles from Capitol Hill, the winter of 1962 also marked the second year of James Madison Nabrit, Jr.'s presidency at Howard University. An article in the January 13, 1962, issue of the *Saturday Evening Post,* "Our Negro Aristocracy," had reignited Thompson's interest in charting the political and economic status of African Americans. In this article, the journalist Bill Davidson claimed to have found a large African American "leisure class" with pretensions similar to those whites who had also acquired "more wealth than one knows what to do with" purchasing "yachts, ornate mansions in the middle of 10 acre lots, racing stables, and all the other claptrap." Thompson considered this development auspicious for several reasons, the least of which was that a few African Americans had managed to acquire astronomical wealth despite adverse circumstances. The existence of wealthy African Americans was notable for Thompson because it freed these primarily middle-class professionals such as himself to devote their full energies and attention to the struggle for civil rights.[1]

Thompson was prompted by Davidson's article to search the 1960 Census for more meaningful data on African Americans' standing in US society. He found that there were 18,871,831 African Americans, totaling 10.5 percent of the American population, which was 179,831,732 persons. As an identifiable group, African Americans were younger and their numbers had grown at a faster rate than any other segment of the US population, so that they would comprise 11 percent of the US population by 1970 if the current trends prevailed. According to the Census, fewer than one million persons in the United States identified themselves as Indian or Japanese, and fewer than 750,000 identified themselves as Chinese, Filipino, or nonwhite. Thompson pointed out that African

Americans outnumbered the population of Canada; every nation in South America with the exception of Mexico, Argentina, and Brazil; and every nation in Africa with the exception of Egypt, Ethiopia, and Nigeria.[2]

The leaders of US corporations and businesses had tailored their advertising campaigns to capture a major segment of the African American market, which was then estimated at twenty billion dollars annually, and in describing these "unprecedented" advertising campaigns Thompson also noted some of the material benefits of desegregation:

> Practically every Negro newspaper and magazine of national circulation now carries advertisements of products never before advertised in these media, and except for the use of Negro models such advertisements are indistinguishable from those carried by similar national news media. Moreover, many national distribution agencies have employed Negro representatives and [salespeople] on an unprecedented scale, even for whiskey, beer, soft drinks, and cigarettes.[3]

In 1960, conservative estimates of the African American market set its value at more than half of the United States' worldwide exports in 1959, double US exports to Europe, and more than three times US trade with either Canada, South America, or Asia. This realization shifted Thompson's concern to the nagging problem of income inequality in the United States and the racial and economic discrimination that he thought responsible for fueling that disparity. Noting that the educational attainment of African Americans was about 70 percent of that of whites in the United States, but that instead of earning 70 percent of the income African American families earned only "55.4 percent as much as the average income for the white family, despite the fact that the Negro family was 20 percent larger,"[4] Thompson estimated this difference of $2.8 billion to be the result of racial discrimination and he traced its roots as follows:

> Income is inextricably bound up with educational level and fair employment opportunity. Negroes, perennially—although less now than formerly—have been denied equitable educational opportunity, excluded in large numbers from certain types of better-paid jobs, and even where a few have obtained better-paid jobs they have received promotion on merit most infrequently or not at all—certainly not as frequently as they deserved.[5]

Accordingly, his winter 1962 editorial, "The Relative Significance of the Negro Population in the United States," was intended to highlight the persistent lack of knowledge about "the present status and future possibilities of the Negro race in America," and for this reason he called for "a series of comprehensive studies" on the scale of Gunner Myrdal's classic study, *An American Dilemma: The Negro Problem and Modern Democ-*

racy (1944) in anticipation of "the 100th anniversary of the Emancipation [Proclamation] in 1963."[6]

A few months later, in the spring of 1962, Thompson paused to recognize the formal end of the era of dual standards in accrediting the African American colleges in the South, which had occurred at the annual meeting of the Southern Association of Colleges and Secondary Schools at Miami Beach, Florida on December 7, 1961, recognizing its standards approved in December 1957. Thompson attributed this result to the agency exercised by the leaders of African American higher education in the South, who had assumed the risks of reevaluating more than half of the sixty-six institutions of higher learning that had failed to qualify for full accreditation in 1956. By early December 1961 fifty, or slightly more than 75 percent, of these African American colleges in the South earned full regional accreditation, and thirteen of the sixteen African American colleges that had been denied accreditation were private or church-related historically black colleges and universities. Three African American public colleges in the South also failed to earn regional accreditation in December 1961. Thompson noted that in contrast to the three-fourths of the four-year African American colleges that the Southern Association approved for regional accreditation, only 15 percent of the thirty-three African American community colleges in the South received that designation, compared to nearly 80 percent of the community colleges serving white youth. Thompson pointed out that as deplorable as this situation was, African American high schools still suffered from the Southern Association's insistence on applying dual accreditation standards, and he expressed the hope that having now abandoned this practice in higher education, the Southern Association soon would accredit more African American secondary schools. It concerned Thompson that in 1962 considerable numbers of both white and African American youth in the South had attended high schools that were not accredited. There was nonetheless wide variation among these high schools, with 45 to 60 percent of Southern white youth attending regionally accredited high schools as opposed to 15 to 45 percent of their African American contemporaries. Desiring more information about this stark inequality, Thompson called for "a careful study . . . of the number and caliber of high schools and graduates [in the South because of the importance of that data for] the future of higher education in the region" and educational policymaking.[7]

Upon publication, there were no detectable signs that *The Negro Public College*, the 1962 issue of the Yearbook, would be Thompson's last, especially because his renewed focus on the African American public college was a logical follow-up to his spring 1962 editorial, "The Southern Association and the Predominately Negro College and High School." In that editorial, Thompson had noted that three African American public colleges—Alabama State College, Alabama Agricultural and Mechanical College, and Mississippi Vocational College—had not met the standards for earning regional accreditation in 1962.[8] Moreover, because the academic year 1962/1963 marked the centennial of the founding of the land-grant colleges in the United States, *The Negro Public College* served to evaluate this sector. The forty-eight African American public colleges in the South served 58,616 students in 1960/1961, and they also accounted for 20 percent of the number of publicly supported higher education institutions in the South at this time.[9] Despite the continuing resistance to desegregation, these African American public colleges would ultimately have to justify their existence in terms of their capacity for delivering results related to the region's needs for higher education as well as its economic objectives.

One of the primary purposes of *The Negro Public College* was forecasting the most profitable "future role [of African American public colleges in the South]," but Thompson also designed this Yearbook to uncover the most urgent problems facing this subset of institutions.[10] Therefore, Thompson had one section of the 1962 Yearbook function as a survey of comparable data that would permit these colleges to survive when higher education in the South entered more fully into the era of desegregation.[11] The first section traced the history of public higher education in the United States and provided the social context of the launch of African American public higher education shortly before the Civil War.[12] The second section presented a series of case studies that highlighted the problems and opportunities confronting African American public colleges in the Southern states that had not permitted desegregated public education before May 17, 1954. The third section, "The Present Status and Future Role of the Negro Public College," offered recommendations for bolstering the performance of the African American public colleges, land-grant colleges, community colleges, and teacher-training colleges, additionally identifying niche markets for these institutions as higher education in the United States entered a period of uncertainty and turbulence. This section also offered guidance for these colleges to "serve more effectively the educational needs of the state" as the "desegregation of higher education" in the South became an accomplished fact.[13]

A subsidiary question resonating throughout the 1962 Yearbook was the extent to which the Southern states had fulfilled their higher educational obligations as defined by the Supreme Court's rulings in *Gaines* (1938), *Sweatt* (1950), *McLaurin* (1950), and *Brown* (1954 and 1955). This yearbook shared the defining characteristic of Thompson's other publications: its pages blended the voices and insights of different generations of African American scholars, including younger scholars such as Hurley H. Doddy and Carroll L. Miller, senior scholars such as Walter G. Daniel and L. D. Reddick, and even older predecessors such as John Warren Davis of whom Thompson had noted in a letter dated September 22, 1961, that a request for a chapter would be forthcoming. In his essay, "The Status of the Negro Public College: A Statistical Summary," Hurley H. Doddy, associate professor of education at Howard University, acknowledged the Southern states' investments in public higher education to the tune of three billion dollars in facilities and equipment, spending a billion dollars annually but not committing much of this to furthering equity, or justice.[14] Doddy captured the situation by noting:

> It is a picture of 10 per cent of the population attending 5 per cent of the institutions run on about 2 per cent of the resources spent on physical plant and general operation. In almost all categories of accounting these . . . Negro institutions were spending and receiving far less per student than were the other institutions as a group.[15]

Doddy also documented how the higher education policies enacted by the Southern states had served to reinforce educational discrimination while worsening the resulting inequality, his research confirming that the two types of educational discrimination that had been pervasive during the era of segregation persisted years after the mandate to desegregate. Thus, as late as 1962 very little desegregation had occurred in the South, and many of the public universities, colleges, and junior colleges in the region enrolled only Southern whites. So lopsided was this expenditure that Doddy concluded that it effectively increased the considerable competitive advantage that the region's formerly white public colleges and universities had garnered during the era of segregation. These data compelled Doddy to observe:

> the state of the Negro institutions supported by public funds reveal that they are far behind in almost every respect. They have less invested in physical plant and equipment, spend less on current operations, have faculties with a smaller proportion of Ph.D.'s, inadequate libraries, limited scope of program, and trying to do some work at graduate level without adequate resources. [The Southern states could remedy] many of these conditions . . . with greater financial support. The consequence of discrimination in public support of Negro institutions of higher education forces upon [the African American public colleges] the task of trying to educate with less of everything necessary to conducting adequate educational programs.[16]

Moreover, Doddy corroborated the continuation of the Southern states' widespread practice of "double taxation" of their African American residents. Whereas African Americans paid their fair share, the continued enforcement of segregation policies effectively excluded African Americans from the benefits purchased by their tax dollars, and they had to rely much more heavily on expensive private colleges for undergraduate education than did Southern whites. Thus, Doddy predicted that African American public colleges were:

> destined to remain far behind and inadequate. Their relative position now is weak compared with white public institutions. Much of the progress made in the past decade in these institutions was the result of

> threatened integration and efforts to forestall integration. Such effort did little to close the gap which developed over a long period of time. With integration policy established in many states through initial cases, the relative status of the schools is likely to be unchanged. Until such time as these institutions receive adequate support in all areas, any serious discussion of providing quality education seems premature. Quality is something achieved after the necessities have been supplied. These states have failed to provide for the necessary elements of adequate higher education for Negroes.[17]

Building on this theme in his essay, "The Negro Publicly-Supported Junior College," Carroll L. Miller documented the South's need for additional four-year and two-year public colleges, suggesting that its economy would grow much faster if its leaders abandoned segregation and provided the region's African American citizens with the education necessary to realizing their potential. The evidence that Miller documented showed that Southern white leaders were not inclined to support progressive, racially neutral policies, but considered publicly supported two-year colleges as an opportunity for ensuring that African Americans remained at the bottom of the region's racially differentiated economy. In his essay, Miller further reported that in the South educational leaders had intentionally duplicated segregated, publicly supported two-year colleges in the same community, one for whites and the other for African Americans. Although these colleges appeared to be "separate but equal" on the surface, a closer examination revealed them to be as segregated and as unequal as was humanly possible.[18] For example, in Florida:

> As one looks at the junior colleges serving Citrus, Levy and Marion Counties, one observes an emphasis on business education and secretarial science at Central Junior College (White) at Ocala and two programs, cosmetology and food service administration at Hampton Junior College (Negro) at Ocala. In Pinellas County, St. Petersburg Junior College (White) lists five terminal programs: business, clerical specialist, dental hygiene, food service and police administration and public safety; whereas Gibbs Junior College (Negro) indicates that a 2-year secretarial course, 1-year secretarial skills course, and a 2-year nursery-kindergarten education program represent the breadth of its terminal program. . . . It is noted then that in the dual junior college set-up in Florida counties, the publicly controlled junior colleges which enroll Negro students have limited terminal programs which tend to perpetuate job placements in low level positions and which offer no opportunities for Negro youth to break into the newly opened fields of technology.[19]

Moreover, not only had the South's educational leaders authorized the provision of grossly inferior educational opportunities for their African American schools, but they had also severely limited this schooling: Miller reported that the secondary school training of African

American students in the region was, in fact, what Southern whites received in "the upper levels of elementary schools."[20] This led Miller to conclude that such disparities would persist until Southerners compelled their school officials to fulfill their responsibilities more democratically, and thereby permit the African American public two-year colleges to perform their duties for adult education as well as act as incubators for the development of African American communities and neighborhoods.

In his essay, "Liberal Arts and Teacher Education in the Negro Public College," Walter G. Daniel, a professor of education at Howard University, recommended six reforms to strengthen the African American public colleges and bolster their chances of survival. In recognition of the fact that many first-year, African American college students were unprepared to succeed, Daniel called for comprehensive and intensive programs of remediation to be provided for them upon enrollment covering the writing, speaking, reasoning, and analytical skills that they lacked, in addition to "softer" skills such as self-management, resilience, and self-motivation. In a similar vein, Daniel recommended a thorough revamping of the African American public colleges' curricula to emphasize instruction in African American history and psychology courses to prepare these students to deal proactively with racism and their minority status so that self-discovery and intellectual growth would become essential outcomes of their college expectations. Daniel further asserted:

> Education is the only means thus far devised for dealing competently with the problems of people, the creating of a sense of society or community, or the fulfillment of individual potential and well-being. Education becomes essential for both majority and minority members who must learn to solve the problems of their relationship in a multi-group society. The public colleges must assume their responsibility for utilizing higher education to help with these problems.[21]

Daniel also focused on creating and expanding the opportunities for interdisciplinary study in the liberal arts, "business, home economics, or nursing, as well as teaching," believing that these subjects offered opportunities for the "synthesis, coordination or integration of educational experiences" in ways that might better prepare students for the demands of a modern, non-segregated economy. He sought to foster students' sense of professionalism, discipline, and preparation, particularly in new fields that emphasized technical qualifications.[22] On the other hand, in 1962, the pressing need for improving teachers and teaching required the colleges to engage more talented faculty, which in turn involved providing competitive salaries, attractive working conditions, and intellectually and culturally stimulating environments, travel to professional meetings, and increased "contacts with libraries, laboratories, and research facilities" to facilitate the fulfillment of their research agendas.[23] Daniel was confident that if these colleges became more attractive to talented scholars and students, their visibility and stature would increase, and that their survival would benefit from continuous self-examination. He pointed out that although the impediments to conducting self-studies were few, the rewards were many:

> Each institution can begin a serious self-study; each one can project itself beyond the objective of meeting minimum standards of accreditation; each can secure the help of competent, professional people to assist in evaluation and program planning; and all can remain true to the ideals of service to people, state, and nation as conceived by their founders.[24]

The historian Lawrence Dunbar Reddick in his 1962 Yearbook essay, "Critical Review: The Politics of Desegregation," focused on defining the methods for accomplishing the objectives that Daniel had so persuasively articulated. He argued that the success of the African American public college depended upon the agency of African Americans and "the strength and will of the Negro community." Roy Wilkins had advocated for these factors in the 1957 issue of the Yearbook, and Reddick agreed that the problems that limited equal educational opportunity for African Americans were actually political issues that demanded old-fashioned, political solutions. Reddick, therefore, proposed a return to the multifaceted and orchestrated political movement that would involve members of the press, scholars engaged in policy research, community organizers who directed the nonviolent protest efforts, and lawyers engaged in litigation who had produced the successes represented by the *Brown* decisions and the victorious Montgomery bus boycott. However, Reddick believed that political realities in the hard-core states such as Alabama and Mississippi had made it necessary for African American educators to pursue policy goals that were not appropriate in states such as Maryland where some desegregation had occurred. Accordingly, he urged African Americans and their allies to press for complete equality in "plant investment and equipment, operational income, salaries . . . courses and services" in the states maintaining segregation, but to concentrate on pushing politicians to ensure that the African American public colleges were first-rate institutions in their states' systems of higher education where some desegregation had occurred.[25] Reddick believed that an informed, aroused, and unified African American community could ensure the survival of African American public higher education if it made that goal its top priority, noting the successes of African Americans and their allies in Oklahoma and Delaware:

> applying the weight of Negro intellectuals, voters and taxpayers . . . on the side of retaining institutions that are now operating under Negro leadership and building them into colleges of such excellence that any but the most prejudiced will be glad to attend them.[26]

Reddick was not alone among the contributors to the 1962 Yearbook in concluding that the synthesis of policy research, litigation, nonviolent protest, lobbying, and practical politics was still a viable method for expanding equity and social justice in these United States. In a sense, the 1962 issue of the Yearbook, *The Negro Public College*, served as a proxy for a reassessment of the strategy that had yielded the *Brown* decision. This blueprint was one of the gifts that Thompson left to his successors, but it must be noted that he expected these scholars who followed him to revise, rewrite, extend, and build on it until human rights were recognized and protected in all quarters of the globe.

NOTES

1. Charles H. Thompson, "Editorial Comment: The Relative Significance of the Negro Population in the United States," *The Journal of Negro Education*, 31, no. 1 (Winter 1962): 1.
2. Ibid., 2.
3. Ibid.
4. Ibid., 3.
5. Ibid.
6. Ibid.
7. Charles H. Thompson, "Editorial Comment: The Southern Association and the Predominately Negro High School and College," *The Journal of Negro Education*, 31, no. 2 (Spring 1962): 107. In the spring 1962 issue, Thompson published Theresa B. Wilkins' tribute acknowledging the contributions of "Ambrose Caliver: Distinguished Civil Servant." As a dean at Fisk University in the 1920s, Dr. Caliver's leadership was instrumental in the accreditation of Fisk University by the Southern Association. In fall 1930, Howard University released Caliver from his faculty contract so he could accept a position as "Specialist in Negro Education in the Office of Education, then a unit of the United States Department of the Interior" on September 2, 1930. Caliver rose steadily up the leadership ranks at the US Office of Education (he served as assistant to the Commissioner, US Office of Education [1950] and won promotion to chief, Adult Education Section, US Office of Education in 1955). His support, contacts, and access to pertinent information were invaluable to Thompson's *Journal*. The two scholars maintained a productive partnership of nearly thirty-two years despite their disagreements regarding the educational value of racially segregated public education. In fact, from 1938 to 1948, Caliver served as a lecturer at Howard University. Ambrose Caliver died suddenly on January 29, 1962, at his home in Washington, DC. See Theresa B. Wilkins, "Ambrose Caliver: Distinguished Civil Servant," *The Journal of Negro Education*, 31, no. 2 (Spring 1962): 212–14.
8. Thompson, "The Southern Association and the Predominately Negro High School and College," 106.
9. Charles H. Thompson, "Editorial Note: The Negro Public College," *The Journal of Negro Education*, 31, no. 3 (Summer 1962): 217.
10. Ibid., 215.
11. Ibid.
12. Hurley H. Doddy, "The Status of the Negro Public College: A Statistical Summary," *The Journal of Negro Education*, 31, no. 3 (Summer 1962): 370.
13. Thompson, "The Negro Public College," 219.
14. Doddy, "The Status of the Negro Public College," 372.
15. Ibid., 371–72.
16. Ibid., 379.

17. Ibid.
18. Carroll L. Miller, "The Negro Publicly-Supported Junior College," *The Journal of Negro Education*, 31, no. 3 (Summer 1962): 387.
19. Ibid., 390–91.
20. Ibid., 394.
21. Walter G. Daniel, "Liberal Arts and Teacher Education in the Negro Public College," *The Journal of Negro Education*, 31, no. 3 (Summer 1962): 411.
22. Ibid., 412.
23. Ibid.
24. Ibid., 413.
25. L. D. Reddick, "Critical Review: The Politics of Desegregation," *The Journal of Negro Education*, 31, no. 3 (Summer 1962): 417.
26. Ibid., 420.

ELEVEN

Where Does the North Star Go at Daybreak?

In the final year of his editorship of the *Journal*, Thompson dealt with the premature deaths of two people whose friendship and talent he had prized. The sociologist and social critic E. Franklin Frazier had died on May 17, 1962, on the eighth anniversary of the *Brown* decision, while *The Negro Public College* was still in development. Labeled as a radical and noted for his campaigns in opposition to police brutality in the nation's capital in the 1950s, Frazier "was attacked as a subversive and harassed by the FBI until his death."[1] Frazier was a friend and colleague, and the two scholars had often shared an office in Howard University's Douglass Hall, but the October 1962 death of Marion Thompson Wright, a professor of education, represented a greater blow, affecting Thompson's and James Madison Nabrit's project of making Howard University a first-class university. In lieu of his usual editorial for the *Journal*'s autumn 1962 issue, Thompson asked Arthur P. Davis, a professor of English who was a noted writer, anthologist, and literary scholar, to prepare an assessment of Frazier's life and career. Thompson had previously extended this recognition to only four distinguished US educators: John Hope, Thomas Jesse Jones, Carter Godwin Woodson who had pioneered African American history as a scholarly specialization, and Booker T. Washington. Thompson added a note to Davis' autumn 1962 editorial, "E. Franklin Frazier (1894–1962): A Profile," describing Frazier as not only a colleague, but also a "distinguished sociologist, and world scholar" and explaining that Davis was "presently engaged in writing a biography of the late Dr. Frazier."[2] Davis' essay pointed out that:

> Frazier spent a great part of his life fighting three things: American racial injustice; the Negro's reluctance to measure up to national stan-

> dards; and the shallowness, pretentions, and false ideals of the black middle class. During his long academic career [spanning forty-five years] he had one overall aim—to tell the truth about racial matters in America. Objective, aggressive, iconoclastic on occasion, he attacked shoddiness and 'foolishness' (his favorite word) wherever he found them. . . . Whatever else he may have been, he was always an honest, forthright, and hard-hitting defender of the things in which he believed. . . . a man of firm convictions . . . [who] feared neither Mrs. Grundy nor the FBI.[3]

He explained that during his undergraduate years at Howard University, Frazier had enjoyed studying with scholars whose "firmness" and "precision" had impressed him, such as "David Houston in English, George M. Lightfoot in Latin, E. P. Davis in Greek, and Carl Murphy in German."[4] This work at Howard University had provided the bedrock upon which Frazier had added an A.M. in sociology at Clark University and a Ph.D. in sociology at Chicago, a university whose "bigness" had inspired warmth and affection in Frazier. After a stint of teaching at Atlanta University and Fisk University, Frazier had returned to his alma mater in 1934 where he joined:

> a group of brilliant young Negro intellectuals—a group that gave the University an academic and intellectual climate that no other Negro school had. These young scholars, like Frazier, were nonconformists and gadflies. They needled the administration on occasion, but they helped to make Howard into a "modern" educational center. Frazier became a very active and influential member of this group. But he was never a blind follower of any one camp, and he criticized his colleagues as readily as he criticized deans and presidents.[5]

Frazier had been among the first to see value in African Studies, and he became a strong advocate of the African Program and of the integration of African Studies into Howard University's curriculum. His course, Sociology 198, "The Negro in America," was not only popular with students but his lectures attracted many auditors. A student tribute published in *The Hilltop*, the Howard University student newspaper, described Frazier as follows:

> He knew his people. He knew their sufferings, their frustrations, and their weaknesses. In his class, the Howard students met themselves, often for the first time. He had anger for the sufferings, sympathy for the frustrations, and ironic stinging ridicule for the affectations and weaknesses of his people.[6]

Davis also noted that Frazier's winning ways with college students extended beyond Howard University:

> When [Frazier] lectured at New York University, his classes gave him a standing ovation at the end of each hour. The Howard students who

> knew him had a deep veneration for Frazier which they expressed by presenting a lecture series in his honor, March 13, 14, 15, 1962.[7]

A family man who was married to Marie Ellen Brown Frazier for forty years, Frazier:

> was proud of his two works on the family. He believed that his study of the subject broke away from the conventional approach and emphasized other aspects of the family, economic, political, religious, as well as social. He tried to write, not the history of the family but the "natural history," a conceptualized showing of stages in the growth of the family unit. *The Annals of the American Academy of Political and Social Science* (January 1940) [called] *The Negro Family in the United States*, "a most important contribution to the literature on the family." [Frazier's] *Negro in the United States* [was] a scholarly and complete survey of the Negro in America from his first appearance here down to the present.' *The Library Journal* (June 1, 1949) considered this work "more up-to-date and factual than *American Dilemma*, far wider in scope than *Black Metropolis* and quite worthy to stand beside these two classics in the field." . . . The consensus of most critics: it [was] a monumental work of scholarship.[8]

Toward the end of his essay, Davis acknowledged that Frazier had presented a study in contrasts. On the one hand, he:

> Could be easily aroused to anger by even the slightest suggestion of disagreement, and yet he was fundamentally a warmhearted and kindly man. When one came to know him, one discovered that his anger was directed toward issues rather than persons. . . . Frazier had a rich sense of humor and was an excellent raconteur and mimic. A peculiar mixture of scholar and social person, he liked good parties, good company, good food, and good drink. Before his illness, he could give an excellent account of himself as a trencherman. After he published *Black Bourgeoisie* one of his friends complained to him: "Ed Frazier, why do you write all this stuff about us black middle class folk when you do the same things?" "You are quite right," said Frazier, "that is why I write so truthfully about such things. I *am* a black bourgeois."[9]

Nonetheless, the campus milieu and the broader community in which Frazier and Thompson had thrived were not as receptive or supportive of talented African American women, as the experiences of Marion Thompson Wright indicated. In the *Journal*'s summer 1963 issue, the last of Thompson's editorship, Walter Daniel Green found it necessary to point out, in "A Tribute to Marion Thompson Wright," that her peers at Howard University had quickly regarded her as a scholar. Moreover, Wright had lived up to their assessment by majoring in sociology and graduating magna cum laude in 1927 and completing her master's degree in education in 1928. During the Great Depression, she had not only financed her own higher education but had also supported a family, being the single parent of two children by obtaining jobs at the Newark

Department of Welfare and, later, the New Jersey State Emergency Relief Organization "as a family visitor, senior case worker, and case supervisor."[10] Marion Thompson Wright was the first African American woman to earn the PhD in history (Columbia, 1940), and her work was so distinguished that the acclaimed historian Horace Mann Bond in his review of Wright's dissertation, "The Education of Negroes in New Jersey," had written:

> This volume is a significant contribution to the literature of a number of fields. The method will commend itself to the critical historian of the wide field of American culture, and the calm and dispassionate exposition unearths material which will be useful to students of social trends as well as educational institutions. Dr. Wright's style is liquid, and would be acceptable in a volume of lighter theme. In a doctoral thesis, her style is nothing short of possessing distinction.[11]

Wright acknowledged her intellectual indebtedness to historian Merle Curti, but Thompson not only regarded her as his protégé: he proved to be one of her most indefatigable champions, according to Thompson's protégé, professor of education, and dean of the Graduate School at Howard University, Dr. Carroll L. Miller.[12] Despite these gifts, "the slings and arrows of outrageous fortune" had taken their toll and:

> Despite being academically successful, Wright's personal life was lonely. She had strained relationships with her children and family members. These issues, which she felt were caused by alienation she felt as an African American and woman scholar in a white and academically male-dominated world, contributed to her death by suicide on October 26, 1962, at the age of sixty.[13]

Her leadership and scholarship were pivotal to the development of the university-wide Counseling Service at Howard University and the university's work in remedial education. In addition to her contributions to research, teaching, and service, Wright's humanity made an impression, and Daniel noted:

> Beyond the professional concerns, [Wright] possessed a rare capacity for friendship. Great empathy enabled her to recognize the needs of a widening circle of friends, to extend a helping hand, to give a word of encouragement, to make a constructive suggestion, to contrive an opportunity for relaxation, or to suggest a new perspective on a pressing problem. Time, energy, devotion, and resources were generously shared. [Wright described her motivation as follows:] "It has been my aim to reflect credit upon my institution and to have some situation improved or some person happier as a result of my effort or influence. In other words—It is my desire to do some good thing every day."[14]

The centennial of the Emancipation Proclamation provided Thompson with a theme for his winter 1963 editorial, "The Centennial of the Emancipation Proclamation," which focused on the nation's commitment to civil rights. In this editorial, Thompson reprinted the text of both the preliminary proclamation that Lincoln had issued on September 22, 1862, and the final Emancipation Proclamation that he had issued on January 1, 1863. The tone of the preliminary proclamation had been conciliatory: Lincoln had not only recognized the property rights of slaveholders, but he proved amenable, after the end of hostilities, to having the federal government compensate those slaveholders who remained loyal to the Union and had voluntarily agreed to abolish slavery. Lincoln had also supported the voluntary removal, relocation, or colonization of the ex-slaves outside of the United States. He had subsequently issued the binding Emancipation Proclamation that limited the abolition of slavery to "the States and parts of States wherein the people thereof respectively [were on January 1, 1863] in rebellion against the United States."[15] Justifying this action on the grounds of "military necessity," Lincoln had also confirmed his decision to admit African Americans "into the armed service of the United States to garrison forts, positions, stations, and other places, and to man vessels of all sorts in said service."[16]

When they were prosecuting the war, Northerners had recognized economic and political concerns, and they had framed the conflict as involving only the preservation of the Union. If they could maintain the Union intact without taking that step, the Northern politicians would have refused to abolish slavery, and to make sure that they had communicated their intentions clearly, they had also rejected the "many free Negroes in Northern cities [who] offered their services as volunteers [to the US army] in the early stages of the conflict."[17] Thompson believed that at the onset of the Civil War, that public opinion in the North, as well as the South, overwhelmingly supported white supremacy, but that the parties had split over whether the South's "agrarian feudalism" or the North's "industrial capitalism" would rule the economy, courts, and politics. Nonetheless, the persistent agitation of abolitionists such as Sojourner Truth, Harriet Tubman, Frederick Douglass, and William Lloyd Garrison had in time reframed the Civil War as a humanitarian conflict whereby limiting the abolition of slavery for reasons of military necessity became acceptable. In January 1963, Thompson felt that those African American celebrants who mistook Lincoln's 1863 Emancipation Proclamation for the Thirteenth Amendment that abolished slavery in the United States and was ratified on December 6, 1865, would profit from rereading "the history of the power struggle which is euphemistically called the Civil War, and Reconstruction."[18] He believed that a reward for their efforts would be the realization that whether Lincoln had recognized it or not, the agency and persistence of African American and white abolitionists had encouraged their commander in chief to pry open the policy window that allowed larger conceptions of freedom to enter. In this vein, Thompson pointed out:

> That [Lincoln's Emancipation Proclamation] did not go as far as some people thought it should have gone, or was motivated more by military necessity than humanitarian concern, [did] not mean that it had little or no significance. It suggested that the conflict which began as a "white man's war" to save the Union, was on its way to being changed to a struggle to free upward of four million slaves, with the indispensable aid of 186,000 black soldiers.[19]

In this essay, Thompson identified African Americans' agency, persistence, and the ability to win friends, while responding to threats and opportunities, as essential elements of what he deemed "the price of freedom." He suggested that African Americans needed to develop a political consciousness based on a sound understanding of African American, US, and world history that would allow them to prosecute their struggle for civil rights during successive generations, and that this would be necessary for them to gain equality. In the winter of 1963, Thompson's reading of history led him to one unassailable conclusion: "whatever progress the Negro has made in attaining even a legal status of equality has been due to political expediency on the one hand and a few unequivocal equalitarians like Charles Sumner, on the other."[20]

In his last *Journal* editorial, Thompson summed up the model of leadership that had advanced his work in becoming the leading dean in African American higher education during the era of segregation and the onset of the age of desegregation. In October 1935, Thompson had saluted the historian Carter G. Woodson for funding *The Journal of Negro History* almost entirely on donations and membership dues from African Americans. Nonetheless, decades later, Thompson proved to have been resistant to following the advice that he had given to Woodson when he encouraged him to select and train a successor to ensure the continuation of *The Journal of Negro History*. Woodson had started with a deficit, and yet he had built the Association for the Study of Negro Life and History into a self-sustaining organization controlled by African American educators; nonetheless, Thompson had then pointed out, "future progress of the Negro and Negro institutions is going to depend upon increased control of the policies of their organizations by Negroes. Such control will not be obtained except through increased financial support [by African Americans], 'for he who pays the fiddler, calls the tune.'"[21] Woodson had indeed demonstrated to other African American scholars that "vision, self-sacrifice, and persistence will be rewarded."[22]

As late as September 1961, Thompson had not secured the services of a successor, for he had, like Woodson, "been so busily engaged in building [his *Journal*] and promoting its growth that he [had] not trained someone to take his place."[23] In response to John Warren Davis's query about whether the demands of leading the university's self-study would require Thompson to relinquish his editorial duties, in a letter dated September 22, 1961, Thompson replied, "As to your hope that my new duties and associations will not force me to give up active direction of the *Journal*, may I say I hope the same thing. I shall hang on a little longer while I am trying to induct some of the younger members into the routine of the job."[24] Nonetheless, in late 1962 and early 1963 there was no obvious successor to Thompson, according to the historian Michael R. Winston.[25] Thompson was able to persuade Walter Green Daniel, a professor of education at Howard University and a leading African American educator, to take over the magazine. When Thompson wrote his last editorial, "A Valedictory Note," in summer 1963, he knew that the *Journal* would not only continue, but that its leadership ranks would continue to be fulfilled by the education faculty at the university. Thus, it was with a sense of relief and thanksgiving that he began the essay by documenting the transition:

> The current volume of the *Journal of Negro Education* is the 32nd since it was started in the early thirties. During this entire period the writer has been privileged to serve as its editor. With the publication of the present number he will become editor *emeritus*. Professor Walter G. Daniel of the Department of Education, Howard University, will become the new editor. Dr. Daniel has been a member of the Editorial Board since the *Journal* was started and a frequent contributor over this period. His long association with the *Journal* should fit him well for this new responsibility.[26]

Thompson continued the editorial by briefly assessing the *Journal*'s success in cultivating a coherent literature about African American education and inserting African Americans' perspectives into ongoing policy debates on this subject as well as on African American life more broadly. While acknowledging that his readers would be the final judges of the *Journal*'s relevance, Thompson did not restrain himself from noting, "few if any important proposals or investigations concerning Negro life and education have been made during the past 30 years in which the *Journal* has not been importantly involved."

The *Journal* remained the leading publication in the field of African American education despite the emergence of competitors and a growing interest on the part of editors of mainstream journals to publish African American scholars. Thompson predicted a continuing need for the *Journal* or a similar agent given the corrosive effects of segregation, racism, inequality, and racial discrimination in the United States, asserting:

> Negroes are still isolated from the mainstream of American life, despite token desegregation, and they are the heirs of years of cultural deprivation, educational retardation, and personality devaluation which will take years and much more knowledge than now obtains to overcome.[27]

Thompson then thanked the "more than 1200 *different* individuals [who had] contributed one or more articles or book reviews [to the *Journal* over the years],"[28] noting that it was unusual for "over half of the original Editorial Board" to remain intact, a testament to their steadfastness and support. He recorded his deep gratitude to Mrs. Hortense C. Moon and Mrs. Theresa A. Rector, two assistant editors who had for twenty-nine and two years, respectively, ensured that the *Journal* had "never missed publication of a single issue," an accomplishment in which he took great pride.[29]

Thompson also expressed his boundless appreciation of the contributions of the president and Board of Trustees of Howard University who had provided the office space, clerical staff, and funding for the *Journal*, giving "the editor . . . complete academic freedom in the exercise of his duties" that made his policy research venture possible.[30] In conclusion, Thompson assured his successor that he "shall be glad to cooperate in any way that I can to make [the new editor's] task easier and more fruitful. Moreover, I should like to express the wish that the new editor will have as much cooperation from the general public as I have had."[31]

Charles Henry Thompson had dominated African American higher education for more than thirty years very much as the North Star dominates the sky at night. If the *Journal* had been present during every "important proposal or investigation concerning Negro life and education," it was because Thompson and the members of his social networks had done the "leg work" to make its presence known and felt. During this period, Thompson had meticulously recorded in the *Journal*'s editorial pages the unfolding of the civil rights movement and the centrality of African American education to that struggle. As early as 1934, he had set full equality as the only worthwhile goal for African Americans or any other self-respecting people in the United States, and he had also carved out a major role for African American higher education in this enterprise. As he penned his farewell nearly three decades later, the mobilization for the 1963 March on Washington was entering its final stages, and this event would bring to fruition a movement begun in 1941. Thompson departed with the satisfaction of knowing that his *Journal* was safe and that he had set an excellent example of how much one person can accomplish when they set personal considerations aside, "rolls up her or his sleeves," and joyfully pays the price of freedom.

NOTES

1. "Sociologist E. Franklin Frazier: 1947," Washington Area Spark, accessed October 17, 2017, https://www.flickr.com/photos/washington_area_spark/8662953731.
2. Arthur P. Davis, "E. Franklin Frazier (1894–1962): A Profile," *The Journal of Negro Education*, 31, no. 4 (Autumn 1962): 429.
3. Ibid., 429–30, 435.
4. Ibid., 430.
5. Ibid., 433.
6. Ibid., 434.
7. Ibid., 433.

8. Ibid., 434.
9. Ibid., 435.
10. Walter G. Daniel, "A Tribute to Marion Thompson Wright," *The Journal of Negro Education*, 32, no. 3 (Summer 1963): 308.
11. Ibid., 308–9.
12. Dr. Carroll Lee Liverpool Miller, interview by author, January 23, 1996, Washington, DC.
13. Samuel Momodu, "Marion Thompson Wright (1902–1962), *BlackPast.org Online Encyclopedia*, accessed October 17, 2017, http://www.blackpast.org/aah/wright-marion-thompson-1902-1962.
14. Daniel, "A Tribute to Marion Thompson Wright," 310.
15. Charles H. Thompson, "Editorial Comment: The Centennial of the Emancipation Proclamation," *The Journal of Negro Education*, 32, no. 1 (Winter 1963): 3.
16. Ibid., 3.
17. Ibid., 5.
18. Ibid.
19. Ibid.
20. Ibid.
21. Charles H. Thompson, "Editorial Comment: The Association for the Study of Negro Life and History," *The Journal of Negro Education*, 4, no. 4 (October 1935): 466.
22. Ibid., 466.
23. Ibid., 467.
24. Charles H. Thompson, letter to John Warren Davis, September 22, 1961, School of Education Papers, Moorland-Spingarn Research Center, Howard University Archives, Howard University, Box 1894, *Journal of Negro Education*.
25. Dr. Michael R. Winston, interview by author, April 17, 1996, Silver Spring, MD.
26. Charles H. Thompson, "Editorial Comment: A Valedictory Note," *The Journal of Negro Education*, 32, no. 3 (Summer 1963): 205.
27. Ibid., 206.
28. Ibid.
29. Ibid.
30. Ibid.
31. Ibid., 207.

TWELVE

Afterword

This chapter examines several of the principles that Thompson regularly observed for their continuing relevance in today's social and political climate: indeed, current events bear striking similarities to those of his era, and Thompson's enduring gift might well be proper and fuller appreciation and emulation of his precepts and practices.

FOCUSING ON ISSUES, NOT PERSONALITIES OR SELF-PROMOTION

Today, Thompson is a cipher in American history in part because of his insistence on drawing attention to issues and not personalities, and his talent for publicizing others' accomplishments instead of his own. In October 1940, Thompson explained his editorial stance to the attendees of a symposium on publication sponsored by the Association for the Study of Negro Life and History, humbly indicating that, for him, these responsibilities were matters of moral integrity:

> I think everyone will agree that the editor of a scientific magazine has "a unique opportunity and a profound responsibility." His function assumes, *first*, that he has an insatiable desire to find Truth; *second*, that he knows the Truth when he sees it, and, *third*, that he will be absolutely honest in printing the Truth when it is found. . . . If one has an insatiable desire to find Truth, he does not sit and wait for it to come to him. He goes after it. He finds out what and where research is in progress and who the investigators are. He suggests to embryo scientists what problems need to be attacked and where the gaps in our present knowledge are. Thus, he willingly sacrifices his own ambitions for research and publication in order to motivate and guide others. . . . It goes without saying that the editor of a scientific magazine should

> report with absolute honesty the findings of research "whether or not they agree with tradition," with the findings of colleagues, or with the theories, preconceptions, or prejudices of the editor.[1]

Thompson also disclosed his reasons for using his editorial opinion to guide the development of a coherent policy research literature that would be relevant to the evolving civil rights movement, a practice that was rare then and unfortunately remains an anomaly today:

> I am strongly of the opinion that the editors of many scientific magazines . . . fail to perform an inescapable responsibility by not periodically indicating the status of scientific knowledge in their several fields, evaluating current contributions, suggesting refinements of technique, calling attention to significant problems, and otherwise indicating where the pursuit of Truth may be profitably followed. . . . Thus, it would appear that a forward step could be made by editors of scientific magazines in their roles of "promoters" of research and disseminators of Truth if more of them would assume this very important function which now goes by default.[2]

Within a decade of the *Journal*'s founding, Thompson and his magazine were widely respected, as anthologists Sterling A. Brown, Arthur P. Davis, and Ulysses Lee concluded in their 1941 assessment, when they noted that "[Thompson's] influence upon Negro scholarship has been marked."[3] According to the late Professor Carroll L. Miller, Thompson's reputation for publishing quality work drew scholars to him. It was his practice to read all submissions to the *Journal* and to edit or "red line them," a practice that Thompson alluded to in one of his many exchanges of letters over the years with historian Horace Mann Bond. Thompson refused to publish shoddy material, Professor Miller asserted, but would instead return unacceptable material to its author(s) accompanied by suggested revisions. Throughout his editorship, Thompson's goals were to do what was good for African American education as a whole and, Dr. Miller maintained, to "provide blacks with the data to support a position."[4]

PRACTICE SCHOLARSHIP IN THE PUBLIC INTEREST

Thompson's receptivity to Gunnar Myrdal's *An American Dilemma* illustrates his ability to recognize the truth even when it fell outside the boundaries of convention. Thompson had immediately recognized that Myrdal's study represented a breakthrough in the fight against segregation and the possible opening of a policy window, and he supported Myrdal's recommendations in favor of using the findings of social science research to enhance the human experience—over the objections of leading sociologists of the Chicago School of Sociology such as Robert Ezra Park and William Ogburn. In his spring 1944 editorial comment, "Some Initial Observations on the Carnegie Corporation's Study of the Negro in America," Thompson endorsed the expanded role that Myrdal had proposed for government in protecting African Americans and nonwhites' civil rights. Nearly two decades later, in a May 21, 1962, letter to James Madison Nabrit, Jr., then president of Howard University, Thompson expressed his continuing appreciation of Myrdal's accomplishments in the text that he prepared for Nabrit for "the citation for Gunnar Myrdal who is to receive an honorary degree at the June 1962 commencement [of Howard University]." Thompson's remarks in this citation may be seen as strikingly autobiographical, because his approach to social science research resonated strongly with that espoused by Myrdal:

> Your activities as a scholar and social engineer have been highly unique, if not *sui generis*. You have not been content, as most social scientists, merely to engage in "theoretical" research "directed purely or exclusively toward ascertaining facts and causal relations among facts." But equally, perhaps to a greater extent, you have been vitally interested in "relating value judgments to factual situations and actual trends of change and, from their combination, deriving scientific plans for policies aimed at inducing alterations of the anticipated social trends." It has been within this framework that your most constructive and significant research has been prosecuted, thus freeing you from the proverbial "ivory tower" of most social scientists.[5]

Moreover, as formulated by Thompson, time had not diminished the value of Myrdal's research:

> In this country, the work for which you are best known and acclaimed is your monumental study of "The Negro Problem and Modern Democracy" which you epigrammatically called "An American Dilemma," and succinctly described as a "problem in the heart of the American." This study—involving the participation of almost a hundred investigators—is not only the most comprehensive piece of cooperative social research undertaken in this country, but it is the most definitive and authoritative study of the American Negro ever made. Robert Lynd, distinguished sociologist, characterized it as "the most penetrating and important book on our contemporary American civilization that has ever been written." *An American Dilemma*, despite its heavy emphasis on race relations, is the most perceptive and significant examination of American democracy since de Tocqueville and Bryce. Yours has been a significant contribution not merely to a better way of life for the Negro, but, even more important, to the salvation of America's soul.[6]

Thompson, too, believed firmly in the capacity of scientific reasoning, applied research, and social engineering to enhance the lives of the ordinary people, and it was the fidelity with which he practiced scholarship with an eye to improving the human condition that gives his work its enduring freshness and importance.

A SOUND HISTORICAL UNDERSTANDING IS ESSENTIAL

History has an uncanny way of repeating itself, Thompson often noted, and he felt that it behooved activists to study its lessons carefully and apply those insights when formulating their plans. On the other hand, lacking a sound understanding of history increased the likelihood that injustices would persist. He frequently decried the underrepresentation, and sometimes the absence, of African and African American history in the general education curriculum at Howard University and other leading historically black colleges and universities during the era of segregation and beyond. Based on surveys that Thompson and several colleagues had administered in the late 1950s and early 1960s, he concluded that little distinguished the historical understanding of first-year students from that of seniors at these colleges.[7] Thompson's analyses left him concerned about African American higher education's capacity to help its students deal with racism and the other problems that they would inevitably encounter after graduation.[8] Moreover, he felt that its tendency to adopt mainstream standards uncritically had reduced its effectiveness, while ceding a niche in the crowded US higher educational market that might sustain these institutions as the pace of desegregation quickened.

Two days after the 1960 presidential election, Thompson discussed his continuing concerns that too many African American undergraduates lacked "a world perspective of racial discrimination and injustice which will lift them out of their narrow personal or group frame of reference to a level of genuine concern for universal human rights, irrespective of race, creed, or geography."[9] In his opinion, African American higher education had failed to help its students develop a healthy identity and an optimistic yet realistic outlook on life, and he pointed to the reluctance of too many African American faculty to examine the implications of race and class as contributing to this dilemma in their scholarship. During his editorship, Thompson showcased the work of leading historians such as Howard K. Beale, Horace Mann Bond, W. E. B. Du Bois, John Hope Franklin, Rayford W. Logan, August Meier, Lawrence D. Reddick, Charles H. Wesley, and C. Van Woodward. In fact, the typical Yearbook following his editorial had an introductory section that would be several chapters in length, permitting leading historians and legal scholars to provide the background and social context of the problem under investigation in that issue. Thompson often displayed his knowledge of history and US culture by situating recommendations in his editorial comments in keeping with his interpretation of US history. For example, his restatement of his support for a direct attack on segregation in the courts in fall 1951, as he explained to his readers, declared:

> I have the feeling based upon our past history that the "time is now." During every crisis in our history we tend more toward democracy

> than in "normal" times. I fear that the same reaction will set in after the present tension is eased either by a victorious war with Russia or by engendering a spirit of intolerance due to the feeling of strength upon the successful completion of our defense program. Accordingly, 1951, and 1952 at the latest, is the most propitious time to press this matter to a favorable conclusion. It is my hope that we take full advantage of this opportunity.[10]

Thompson chose as his baseline or benchmark for measuring the progress, or lack of progress, in the education of African Americans, the status of these schools and colleges in the South in 1926. In doing so, he chose a period that many of his readers could vividly recall having experienced segregation and white racism as youths and young adults. Thompson designed the *Journal* to focus on contemporaneous educational history to take advantage of his readers' recollections of the sacrifices their families had made to obtain adequate schooling and their long treks as children to poorly equipped schoolhouses as sleek buses transporting white youth to modern campuses glided pass them. Segregated education (housing, jobs, transportation, and public accommodations) were potent symbols in Afro-America during the era of segregation, and the data that Thompson published in the *Journal* suggested that the deplorable educational conditions that he and his readers had experienced had steadily worsened. Thompson drew upon this recent memory to tap into a spirit or zeitgeist that would motivate and sustain the litigation campaigns and direct action movements in the South as African Americans, having grown tired of injustice, decided to oppose Jim Crow with every legal means at their disposal.

SOCIAL NETWORKING TO STIMULATE THINKING, REFORMS, AND IMPROVEMENTS

Even in his time, Thompson made social networking look easy, but this was not always the case, as several exchanges of letters describing his difficulties in recruiting "competent" authorities for various issues of the *Journal*'s Yearbooks attest. For example, in an October 30, 1959, letter to Horace Mann Bond regarding his proposal and "tentative table of contents outlining the aims and scope" of the 1960 issue of the Yearbook, *The Negro Private and Church-Related College*, Thompson noted that, "Getting competent contributors is always a difficult task, and it is going to be especially true for this Yearbook. I will be especially grateful for any suggestions which you can give us on this point."[11]

Concurring with Thompson's assessment about this difficulty on November 18, 1959, Bond replied, "As you know, there is no more skilled politician that the denominational board officer."[12] Similarly, in his October 25, 1960, letter to Bond regarding the status of the 1961 Yearbook,

African Education South of the Sahara, Thompson wrote, "Thanks very much for your very helpful suggestions in connection with our yearbook on African education. Your suggestions [were] particularly helpful because I have had some difficulty getting this project 'off the ground.'"[13] Nonetheless, Thompson operated on the assumption that there was nothing extraordinary about his approach to identifying potential authors and asking for their support: it merely required persistence, he felt.

As noted earlier, Thompson was a senior faculty member at Howard University, and he and the *Journal*'s advisory editors traveled extensively to regularly participate in professional associations and scholarly society meetings such as those of the American Teachers Association (formerly National Association of Teachers in Colored Schools), the Conference of the Presidents of Negro Land Grant Colleges, and meetings sponsored by various divisions or departments of the National Educational Association. Thompson also maintained memberships in scholarly societies such as the National Society of College Teachers of Education, the National Society for the Study of Education, and the Academy of Political and Social Science. In addition, he was a fellow of the American Association for the Advancement of Science, and he also served as a member of the US National Commission for the UN Educational, Scientific and Cultural Organization in the US Department of State from 1946 to 1949; between 1948 and 1957, he served on the American Council on Education's Committee on Discrimination in Higher Education.[14] His external service often complemented his research and publication agendas while expanding his network of contacts. As dean of the Graduate School at Howard University, Thompson also hired scholars such as Ambrose Caliver and Caroline Ware, whose government positions and access to research and data sponsored by the federal government proved invaluable to Thompson's project.

Thompson did his social networking in person or by using the telephone or personal letters. Moreover, to ensure that the *Journal* remained relevant, Thompson asked his colleagues in higher education, state and federal agencies, and private philanthropic foundations to notify him about promising theses, presentations, or projects, and to inform prospective authors about the *Journal*. Indeed, during his editorship, the magazine regularly featured abstracts and syntheses of new or recent research related to African American education that Ellis O'Neal Knox, professor of education at Howard University, and Dorothy Porter, the noted bibliographer, had compiled. Thompson maintained careful records of his contacts, and he would write to them, for example, noting the date, city, and meeting where he and the correspondent had met, and then extending an invitation to write a three thousand-word essay on a topic within that scholar's expertise. If that person declined, Thompson would ask them in a subsequent letter to suggest other scholars who might be able to fulfill his request.[15]

Thompson also was very generous in sharing his expertise: in a letter to Thompson dated July 17, 1958, the sociologist Lewis Wade Jones of Tuskegee Institute reported:

> Dan Dodson has accepted the idea we felt you out on and has agreed to make the January issue of *The Journal of Educational Sociology* a Special Issue on "Negro Higher Education 1938–1958" in commemoration of the 20th anniversary of the *Gaines* decision. . . . I should very much like to get you to do the "Critique" [Chapter VII: "Prospects of the Negro College"]. If you can squeeze this into your autumn schedule, it would add much to the issue.[16]

In his response dated July 25, 1958, Thompson wrote, "while I have no business promising to do so because of my full schedule, I shall be very glad to attempt it."[17] Regarding the November 10 deadline that Jones had proposed, Thompson suggested: "The time between October 15 [when Thompson was to receive the chapters] and November 10 [when he was to complete his evaluation] is unusually short as you may surmise. I have looked at the proposed Table of Contents and it seems to cover the subject very well."[18] Thompson emphasized producing quality work by the designated deadline, a practice that he regularly followed at the *Journal*, and given this disposition, it was unsurprising for him to remind Jones in a letter dated October 23, 1958,

> I have been waiting patiently since the 15th of October to receive copies of the papers of which I am to make a critical summary. Were the contributors to send them to me directly or were you to collect them and send them to me? I hope that I can get to them soon so I may erase this item off my calendar.[19]

As adept as Thompson was at cultivating external supporters, he also excelled at nurturing faculty within Howard University in his roles as dean of the College of Liberal Arts (1938 to December 1943) and dean of the Graduate School (1944 to 1961). A case in point is the professional relationship that he maintained with Ellis O'Neal Knox, who served as a professor of education at Howard University during Thompson's deanships while also serving as "Assistant Director for the Office of Vocational Education in Washington [1937 to 1945]," adjunct professor at American University [1941], "an adjunct lecturer at Yale, pushing for improvement on minority education," and "the National Chairman of the Education Division of the NAACP from 1940 to 1962."[20]

As if this were not enough, Knox's great-granddaughter, Allison M. Chaney, reported that Knox also supported the "work of Charles H. Houston and Thurgood Marshall in preparation for the *Brown v. the Board of Education* case" in addition to serving as a member of the "President's White House Conference on Education [1955]" and as a "consultant to both the Peace Corps and the U.S. Commission on Civil Rights [1962]." Thompson's ability to retain Knox at Howard shows that, with the aid of the university's leaders, Thompson managed to make Howard University an attractive place of employment for talented faculty members such as Knox in the critical period when US higher education was desegregating and a variety of lucrative employment opportunities were opening up in government, business, as well as mainstream institutions.[21] What Thompson lacked in financial resources he made up in respect, encouragement, and support that reinforced ties to Howard University during a critical period in its history.

LEADING BY PRECEPT AND EXAMPLE

Thompson's students admired him because in him they found a powerful example of what it meant to live "a socially-constructive and a satisfying and worthwhile personal life in a dynamic and ever-changing social order."[22] The significance of the *Brown* decision for US race relations notwithstanding, as late as November 10, 1960, Thompson used the phrase "racially conditioned" to describe African Americans' relationship to the American social order. According to the historian Michael R. Winston, Thompson was one of the psychologically healthiest teachers at Howard University during this period[23] ; he honestly dealt with the indignities associated with white racism while projecting a sense of confidence, strength, and personal integrity that he attributed to his ability to "[achieve] a proper balance between accommodation to the *status quo* and effective protest against it."[24] In November 1960, Thompson implied that issues related to mental health would remain a pressing concern for African Americans despite their recent achievement of legal equality:

> one of the things that has been most ironical to me—particularly since Negroes have begun to make a frontal attack upon segregation, including the recent sit-in demonstrations—has been the extent to which some Negroes, even college-bred Negroes who have some responsibility for example and leadership, voluntarily cooperate with segregation. Such Negroes in my humble opinion have not developed a philosophy of life that will aid them to live with a maximum of dignity and self-respect and a minimum of frustration and self-disesteem in this racially-conditioned society of ours.[25]

As a teacher, Thompson felt that his primary responsibility was to help his students live worthwhile lives. To do so, he built upon the model that he had learned from his mentor Joshua Baker Simpson, the renowned professor of Greek, Latin, literature, and sociology, during his college years at Virginia Union University. Disgusted by the banality and paternalism that he had found to be an integral part of service on interracial committees, Simpson withdrew from external service and confined his formidable talents to the classroom. According to the historian Raymond Gavins, Simpson was among the African American scholars at

Virginia Union University at the turn of the twentieth century who believed that "classroom performance, not outside involvement, was the best route to Negro elevation."[26] Thompson expanded upon Simpson's model by contributing not only in the classrooms of Howard University but also in its highest administrative offices and beyond. In this way, his external service would eventually have an impact on the lives of ordinary African Americans that strict practitioners of Simpson's philosophy never equaled.

Nearly three decades after his graduation from Virginia Union, Thompson reflected on the qualities that had endeared Simpson to him,

> The "Josh Simpson" that I knew had achieved in his own person that intellectual and emotional poise which is the result of a real and dynamic philosophy of life (I think I was most impressed by the character of this man.) He acted as if he knew what was worthwhile in life and lived as if he knew what he wanted from life. There was something Gibraltarish and even contagious about his integrity. He had an uncompromising sense of responsibility. A thing promised was done, done well, and on time. He had the vision to know the right and this without fear of consequences or hope of reward.[27]

THOMPSON: AN ASSESSMENT

There is a temptation to view Thompson's accomplishments using today's standards rather than those of his era. Thompson created a scholarly journal focused on African American education defined broadly, and he skillfully used this forum to mobilize a policy community in opposition to the public policy of racial segregation in US education and the larger society. Beginning with its debut issue in April 1932, the research published in Thompson's *Journal* contributed to lessening inequities in, for example, African American teachers' salaries between 1932 and 1945 by building support for the National Association for the Advancement of Colored People's (NAACP's) litigation campaigns. In the postwar period, Thompson's *Journal* editorials mobilized activists and exhorted them to support not only the NAACP's litigation and voter registrations campaigns but also the direct action movements in the South. The political pressure produced by this combination of litigation, boycotts, and protest marches eventually split the economic and political elites in the South, leading to a reduction in the glaring gaps in the educational opportunities provided by the states to Southern whites and African Americans in the South.

This assessment of Thompson's project begins with the three goals that he set for the *Journal* in his debut editorial comment, "Why a Journal of Negro Education?" Shortly after the publication of the first issue in April 1932, the response of readers—ranging from graduate faculty at the

University of Chicago to civil rights leaders to private foundation executives—was ecstatic. All agreed that Thompson had set a standard of excellence that the editors of mainstream journals would do well to emulate, particularly in his presentation of the supporting statistical data. In less than a decade, Thompson helped to establish the specialization in African American education similar to that which Carter Godwin Woodson had created for African American history, and today, the *Journal* remains one of the outstanding scholarly magazines in the field.

In short, Thompson took the scholarly journal and transformed it into a showcase for policy research with important implications for advancing the African American struggle for civil rights. As he suggested in October 1940, Thompson envisioned a role for the academic magazine editor that was not shared by many editors then or today: after spending the workday earning his livelihood as a full-time college professor and administrator, in his spare time Thompson coaxed a literature related to African American education and culture into existence.

In effect, then, Thompson melded scholarship, activism, high standards, mentoring, and faith to produce this literature with the goal of helping youth and adults in the United States—regardless of race, age, gender, creed, ability, ethnicity, or region—have access to publicly supported education capable of unleashing their potential. Thompson battled the injustices made permissible by racial segregation with every ounce of his being. Thompson's understanding of history told him that the Allies' response to World War I and the race riots and attacks against African Americans and progressives, respectively, that followed in its wake had sown the seeds that resulted in the carnage of World War II; his reading of history also found elites responsible for many of the world's tragedies including scientific racism, slavery, segregation, colonialism, discrimination, and educational inequality. As he spent his life quietly defying the low expectations, "caricature, and slander" typically reserved for African Americans, Thompson also found the wherewithal to focus his formidable intellect and talents upon destroying the legal underpinnings of *de jure* segregation in the United States. Thompson believed that small, well-educated, and well-organized pressure groups could be agencies for positive social change and that African American professionals had an obligation to engage in research and service designed to aid those that were less fortunate than they. He and many other African American scholars of his era looked upon education as a calling, and they fulfilled their duties as part of a consecrated mission rather than an occupation. In a similar vein, Thompson envisioned higher education as a resource for not only driving economic development but, more importantly, for strengthening the social fabric by reducing inequality and social conflict. In fact, he believed that universal public higher education was necessary to sustain democracies. As did many of his contemporaries, Thompson was confident that higher education had prepared him to fulfill the responsibilities of citizenship as well as those of leadership and had the capacity to prepare countless others to fulfill those responsibilities too. Although some ridiculed the faith that Thompson placed in Southern youth, he challenged his contemporaries to recommend another prescription beyond education and youth for reversing the damage done to society by older generations.

To recapitulate, Thompson's teachers and mentors at Virginia Union and Chicago introduced him to logic, the ancient languages, literature, and the social sciences. As he made these arts his own, he also honed the skills and dispositions that made his policy research venture one of the most successful ever attempted in the United States. Thompson did not live to witness the dispatch with which judges would one day permit school and political leaders to gerrymander school districts into small, affluent, racially homogeneous enclaves. However, as early as 1935, he pointed out that educational inequality was a function of moral lapses rather than lack of material wealth. Despite having his entreaties ignored, Thompson remained a staunch advocate of desegregation because he viewed it as a constitutional, and necessary, antidote to the structural racism so deeply embedded in American institutions including the public schools. He implied that equal educational opportunity and inclusivity were more likely to provide security, prosperity, and a lasting peace than systems based on privilege and a "winner-take-all" mentality that justified the sacrifice of the many as the price for enriching a few. Thompson implied that it was irresponsible to classify *Brown* as a failure until the law was fully implemented in spirit as well as in deed.

As he periodically reminded his readers, African Americans and their allies had accomplished much since 1926: yet they had much more work to do to rid American education and society of the specter of racial segregation and inequality. Today, in many ways public education in the United States is as racially segregated as it was in 1953, and the significant progress in desegregating public education in the South in the 1970s has been all but lost. Meanwhile, white Americans' antipathy to desegregation (and equal educational opportunity) has found ingenious means of expression leading to increased public support for using public funds to provide exclusionary and exclusive educational privileges. Thus, Thompson's project is as meaningful today as when he founded the *Journal* in October 1931 to equalize the dual system in the segregated states to such an extent that racially segregated public education became too expensive for those states to sustain. That said, Thompson believed that racial segregation was only one manifestation of inequality; therefore, he predicted that if the society eliminated all vestiges of segregation that inequality and injustice would persist. Nonetheless, he placed his confidence in the capacity of higher education to produce the ethical leaders and citizens with the vision, commitment, and perseverance to slowly erode the public support for inequities in schooling and other aspects of life.

Martin Luther's "A Mighty Fortress is our God" was one of Thompson's favorite hymns, and based on his belief in God and human decency, he was confident that equity in the larger society was attainable. Thompson had a genius for working collaboratively with people, even those holding opposing views. He had the discipline to take setbacks in stride while maintaining a balance between forbearance and impatience. His vision of a better world in the making motivated him to work tirelessly in support of an ideal and movement that would usher an era of unprecedented freedom and opportunity for millions, as the pendulum of justice tipped once more, and for a time, in the direction of greater equity. Having accomplished so much in the space of forty years, Thompson's legacy calls for a renewed fight for social justice using and building upon the precepts that served him so well. His career as a scholar/activist compelled him to conclude that economic, social, and educational equality was the only sound basis of sustaining humanity or the American experiment in democracy at home and abroad.

NOTES

1. Charles H. Thompson, "Truth from the Point of View of the Editor of a Scientific Magazine," *Journal of Negro History*, 25, no. 4 (October 1940): 453–55.
2. Ibid., 454.
3. Sterling A. Brown, Arthur P. Davis, and Ulysses Lee, eds., *The Negro Caravan* (1941; reprint, New York: Arno Press and the New York Times, 1969), 936.
4. Dr. Carroll Lee Liverpool Miller, interview by author, January 23, 1996, Washington, DC.
5. Charles H. Thompson, letter to James M. Nabrit, Jr., May 21, 1962, School of Education Papers, Moorland-Spingarn Research Center, Howard University Archives, Howard University, Box 1894, *Journal of Negro Education*; Charles H. Thompson, "Gunnar Myrdal—Statesman, Scholar, Social Engineer," n.d., School of Education Papers, Moorland-Spingarn Research Center, Howard University Archives, Howard University, Box 1894, *Journal of Negro Education*.
6. Ibid.
7. Charles H. Thompson, "New Frontiers for America's Private Colleges: Teaching and Curriculum Planning," speech, Hampton Institute, the inauguration of President Jerome H. Holland, March 6. 1961, 5, School of Education Papers, Moorland-Spingarn Research Center, Howard University Archives, Howard University, Box 1894, *Journal of Negro Education*.
8. Charles H. Thompson, "They Come for Many Reasons," a paper that was part of a panel presentation, North Carolina College 50th Anniversary Celebration, November 10, 1960, 5, School of Education Papers, Moorland-Spingarn Research Center, Howard University Archives, Howard University, Box 1894, *Journal of Negro Education*.
9. Ibid.
10. Charles H. Thompson, "Editorial Comment: How Imminent is the Outlawing of Segregation," *The Journal of Negro Education*, 20, no. 4 (Autumn 1951): 498.
11. Charles H. Thompson, letter to Horace Mann Bond, October 30, 1959, School of Education Papers, Moorland-Spingarn Research Center, Howard University Archives, Howard University, Box 1894, *Journal of Negro Education*.
12. Horace Mann Bond, letter to Charles H. Thompson, November 18, 1959, School of Education Papers, Moorland-Spingarn Research Center, Howard University Archives, Howard University, Box 1894, *Journal of Negro Education*.

13. Charles H. Thompson, letter to Horace Mann Bond, October 25, 1960, School of Education Papers, Moorland-Spingarn Research Center, Howard University Archives, Howard University, Box 1894, *Journal of Negro Education*.

14. Charles H. Thompson, "Questionnaire Completed and returned to: Mr. Robert C. Cook, Editor, 'Trustees, Presidents, and Deans of American Colleges and Universities, Who's Who in American Education, Inc.," December 26. 1957, School of Education Papers, Moorland-Spingarn Research Center, Howard University Archives, Howard University, Box 1894, *Journal of Negro Education*.

15. Ibid.

16. Lewis Wade Jones, letter to Charles H. Thompson, July 17, 1958, School of Education Papers, Moorland-Spingarn Research Center, Howard University Archives, Howard University, Box 1894, *Journal of Negro Education*.

17. Charles H. Thompson, letter to Lewis Wade Jones, July 25, 1958, School of Education Papers, Moorland-Spingarn Research Center, Howard University Archives, Howard University, Box 1894, *Journal of Negro Education*.

18. Ibid.

19. Charles H. Thompson, letter to Lewis Wade Jones, October 23, 1958, School of Education Papers, Moorland-Spingarn Research Center, Howard University Archives, Howard University, Box 1894, *Journal of Negro Education*.

20. "Ellis Knox: A Pillar for Black Education," Allison M. Chaney, University of Southern California (USC), USC Office of Black Alumni Programs, accessed July 2, 2018, https://aaregistry.org/story/ellis-knox-a-pillar-for-black-education.

21. Ibid.

22. Charles H. Thompson, "They Come for Many Reasons," a paper that was part of a panel presentation, North Carolina College 50th Anniversary Celebration, November 10, 1960, 2, School of Education Papers, Moorland-Spingarn Research Center, Howard University Archives, Howard University, Box 1894, *Journal of Negro Education*.

23. Michael R. Winston, interview by author, April 17, 1996, Silver Spring, MD.

24. Thompson, "They Come for Many Reasons," 6 [italics in the original].

25. Ibid.

26. Raymond Gavins, *The Perils and Prospects of Southern Black Leadership: Gordon Blaine Hancock, 1884–1970* (Durham, NC: Duke University Press, 1993), 30.

27. Henry Jared McGuinn, "Phylon Profile, V: Joshua Baker Simpson," *Phylon (1940–1956)*, 6, no. 3 (third quarter 1945): 223.

Bibliography

ARCHIVES

Moorland-Spingarn Research Center, Howard University
Howard University Archives, Moorland-Spingarn Research Center, Howard University
Schomburg Center for Research in Black Culture

INTERVIEWS

Dr. John H. Bracey, Jr., interview by author, October 2010, Cincinnati, Ohio.
Dr. John Hope Franklin, telephone interview by author, June 21, 1996.
Dr. Carroll Lee Liverpool Miller, interview by author, January 23, 1996, Washington, DC.
Mrs. Theresa Rector, telephone interview by author, June 19, 1996; interview by author, June 1996, Washington, DC.
Dr. Rachel Weddington, interview by author, August 12, 1996, New York City.
Dr. Michael R. Winston, interview by author, April 17, 1996, Silver Spring, Maryland.

SOURCES

Ade Ajayi, J. F. "The Place of African History and Culture in the Process of Nation-Building in Africa South of the Sahara." *The Journal of Negro Education*, 30, no. 3 (Summer 1961): 206–13. https://www.jstor.org/stable/2294307.

Bardolph, Richard. *The Negro Vanguard*. New York: Vintage Books, 1961.

Batchelor, John E. *Race and Education in North Carolina: From Segregation to Desegregation*. Baton Rouge, LA: Louisiana State University Press, 2015.

Bond, Horace Mann. "The Origin and Development of the Negro Church-Related College." *The Journal of Negro Education*, 29, no. 3 (Summer 1960): 217–26. https://www.jstor.org/stable/2293637.

———. "Some Major Educational Problems in Africa South of the Sahara: A Critical Summary." *The Journal of Negro Education*, 30, no. 3 (Summer 1961): 358–64. https://www.jstor.org/stable/2294324.

Breathett, George. "Black Educators and the United States Supreme Court Decision of May 17, 1954 (*Brown versus the Board of Education*)." *The Journal of Negro History*, 68, no. 2 (Spring 1983): 201–8. https://www.jstor.org/stable/2717722.

Brown v. Board of Education of Topeka, 347 US 483 (1954).

Brown v. Board of Education of Topeka, 349 U.S. 294 (1955).

Brown, Sterling A., Arthur P. Davis, and Ulysses Lee, eds. *The Negro Caravan*. New York: Arno Press and the New York Times, 1941; reprint, 1969.

Carter, Robert L., and Thurgood Marshall. "The Meaning and Significance of the Supreme Court Decree on Implementation." *The Journal of Negro Education*, 24, no. 3 (Summer 1955): 397–404. http://www.jstor.org/stable/2293469.

Chaney, Allison M. "Ellis Knox: A Pillar for Black Education." University of Southern California, USC Office of Black Alumni Programs. https://aaregistry.org/story/ellis-knox-a-pillar-for-black-education.

Clark, Felton G. "The Development and Present Status of Publicly-Supported Higher Education of Negroes." *The Journal of Negro Education*, 27, no. 3 (Summer 1958): 221–32. https://www-jstor-org.libaccess.fdu.edu/stable/2293755.

Clark, Kenneth B. "Color, Class, Personality, and Juvenile Delinquency." *The Journal of Negro Education*, 28, no. 3 (Summer 1959): 240–51. https://www.jstor.org/stable/2293104.

Collier-Thomas, Bettye, and V. P. Franklin. *My Soul is a Witness: A Chronology of the Civil Rights Era, 1954–1964*. New York: Henry Holt and Company, 1999.

Cowan, L. Gray. "The Current Political Status and Significance of Africa South of the Sahara." *The Journal of Negro Education*, 30, no. 3 (Summer 1961): 180–92. https://www.jstor.org/stable/2294306.

Daniel, Walter G. "Liberal Arts and Teacher Education in the Negro Public College." *The Journal of Negro Education*, 31, no. 3 (Summer 1962): 404–13. https://www.jstor.org/stable/2293879.

———. "A Tribute to Marion Thompson Wright." *The Journal of Negro Education*, 32, no. 3 (Summer 1963): 308–10. https://www.jstor.org/stable/2294383.

Davis, Arthur P. "E. Franklin Frazier (1894–1962): A Profile." *The Journal of Negro Education*, 31, no. 4 (Autumn 1962): 429–35. https://www.jstor.org/stable/2293961.

Dinerman, Miriam. "Sophia Moses Robison." In *Jewish Women: A Comprehensive Historical Encyclopedia*. March 1, 2009. Jewish Women's Archive. Accessed August 15, 2017. https://jwa.org/encyclopedia/article/robison-sophia-moses.

"Discrimination and the Christian Conscience." *The Journal of Negro Education*, 28, no. 1 (Winter 1959): 66–69. https://www.jstor.org/stable/2293397.

Doddy, Hurley H., and G. Franklin Edwards. "Apprehensions of Negro Teachers Concerning Desegregation in South Carolina." *The Journal of Negro Education*, 24, no. 1 (Winter 1955): 26–43. https://www.jstor.org/stable/2293176.

———. "The Status of the Negro Public College: A Statistical Summary." *The Journal of Negro Education*, 31, no. 3 (Summer 1962): 370–85.
https://www.jstor.org/stable/22938.

Driver, Justin. "Op-Ed: 60 Years Later the Southern Manifesto is as alive as Ever." *Los Angeles Times*, accessed September 21, 2017. http://www.latimes.com/opinion/op-ed/la-oe-0311-driver-southern-manifesto-anniversary-20160311-story.html.

Duffy, James. "Portuguese Africa (Angola and Mozambique): Some Crucial Problems and the Role of Education in Their Resolution." *The Journal of Negro Education*, 30, no. 3 (Summer 1961): 294–301. https://www.jstor.org/stable/2294318.

Emerson, Rupert. "Crucial Problems Involved in Nation-Building in Africa." *The Journal of Negro Education*, 30, no. 3 (Summer 1961): 193–205. https://www.jstor.org/stable/2294307.

Fall, Bernard B. "Education in the Republic of The Congo." *The Journal of Negro Education*, 30, no. 3 (Summer 1961): 266–76. http://www.jstor.org/stable/2294315.

Fleming, Harold C. "Resistance Movements and Racial Desegregation." *The Annals of the American Academy of Political and Social Science*, 304, *Racial Desegregation and Integration* (March 1956): 44–52. http://www.jstor.org/stable/1032106.

Franck, Thomas M. "European Communities in Africa." *The Journal of Negro Education*, 30, no. 3 (Summer 1961): 223–231. https://www.jstor.org/stable/2294310.

Franklin, John Hope. "Desegregation—The South's Newest Dilemma." *The Journal of Negro Education*, 25, no. 2 (Spring 1956): 95–100. http://www.jstor.org/stable/2293567.

Gavins, Raymond. *The Perils and Prospects of Southern Black Leadership: Gordon Blaine Hancock, 1884–1970*. Durham, NC: Duke University Press, 1993.

Gloucester Institute. "The Moton Center." https://www.gloucesterinstitute.org/the-moton-campus.

Irving, Florence B. "The Future of the Negro Voter in the South." *The Journal of Negro Education*, 26, no. 3 (Summer 1957): 390–99. https://www.jstor.org/stable/2293422.

Jenkins, Martin D. "The Future of the Desegregated Negro College: A Critical Summary." *The Journal of Negro Education*, 27, no. 3 (Summer 1958): 419–29. https://www.jstor.org/stable/2293777.

Johnson, Charles S. "Some Significant Social and Educational Implications of the U. S. Supreme Court's Decision." *The Journal of Negro Education*, 23, no. 3 (Summer 1954): 364–71. http://www.jstor.org/stable/2293235.

———. "A Southern Negro's View of the South." *The Journal of Negro Education*, 26, no. 1 (Winter 1957): 4–9. https://www.jstor.org/stable/2293316.

Johnson, Guy B. "Desegregation and the Future of the Negro College: A Critical Summary." *The Journal of Negro Education*, 27, no. 3 (Summer 1958): 430–35. https://www.jstor.org/stable/2293778.

Kingdon, John W. *Agendas, Alternatives, and Public Policies*. Second edition. New York: Longman, 2003.

Kingsley, Karen. "Historic Woodmen of Union Building" [Hot Springs, Arkansas]. In *SAH Archipedia*, edited by Gabrielle Esperdy and Karen Kingsley. Charlottesville: UVaP, 2012.http://sah-archipedia.org/buildings/AR-01-051-0001.

Kluger, Richard. *Simple Justice*. New York: Vintage Books, 1977.

"Lawyers to Confer on sit-down Tactics." *Afro American* (Washington, DC), March 15, 1960. https://news.google.com/newspapers/p/afro?nid=BeIT3YV5QzEC&dat=19600315&printsec=frontpage&hl=en.

Lewis, Hylan. "Juvenile Delinquency Among Negroes—A Critical Summary." *The Journal of Negro Education*, 28, no. 3 (Summer 1959): 371–87. https://www.jstor.org/stable/2293116.

Lohman, Joseph D. "Juvenile Delinquency: A Social Dimension." *The Journal of Negro Education*, 28, no. 3 (Summer 1959): 286–99. https://www.jstor.org/stable/2293108

Long, Howard Hale. "The Relative Learning Capacities of Negroes and Whites." *The Journal of Negro Education*, 26, no. 2 (Spring 1957): 121–34. https://www.jstor.org/stable/2293338.

Lubell, Samuel. "The Future of the Negro Voter in the United States." *The Journal of Negro Education*, 26, no. 3 (Summer 1957): 408–17. https://www.jstor.org/stable/2293424.

Martin, Robert E. "The Struggle for Political Realignment: Review of *Revolt of the Moderates* by Samuel Lubell." *The Journal of Negro Education*, 25, no. 4 (Autumn 1956): 424–25. https://www.jstor.org/stable/2293279.

McCray, John H. "Thugs Fail to frighten Civic Leader." *Afro American* (Washington, DC). December 6, 1955: 1–2. https://news.google.com/newspapers/p/afro?nid=BeIT3YV5QzEC&dat=19551206&printsec=frontpage&hl=en.

McGuinn, Henry Jared. "Phylon Profile, V: Joshua Baker Simpson." *Phylon (1940–1956)*, 6, no. 3 (third quarter 1945): 219–24. https://www.jstor.org/stable/272487.

Miller, Carroll L. "The Negro Publicly-Supported Junior College." *The Journal of Negro Education*, 31, no. 3 (Summer 1962): 386–95. https://www.jstor.org/stable/2293877.

Momodu, Samuel. "Marion Thompson Wright (1902–1962), *BlackPast.org Online Encyclopedia*. Accessed October 17, 2017. http://www.blackpast.org/aah/wright-marion-thompson-1902-1962.

Moon, Henry Lee. "Editorial Comment: The Negro Vote in the Presidential Election of 1956." *The Journal of Negro Education*, 26, no. 3 (Summer 1957): 219–30. https://www.jstor.org/stable/2293404.

Nabrit, Jr., James M. "The Future of the Negro Voter in the South." *The Journal of Negro Education*, 26, no. 3 (Summer 1957): 418–23. https://www.jstor.org/stable/2293425.

———. "Howard University Looks to the Future." *The Journal of Negro Education*, 29, no. 4 (Autumn 1960): 412–20. https://www.jstor.org/stable/2294211.

National Park Service, U.S. Department of the Interior, Hot Springs National Park, Arkansas. "African Americans and the Hot Springs Baths." 1–4. https://www.nps.gov/hosp/learn/historyculture/upload/african_americans.pdf.

Newton, Jim. *Justice for All: Earl Warren and the Nation He Made*. New York: Riverhead Press, 2007.

Osborne, Irene. "Section B: Desegregation of Washington Schools: The First 60 Days." *The Journal of Negro Education*, 24, no. 1 (Winter 1955): 78–86. http://www.jstor.org/stable/2293193.

——— and Richard K. Bennett. "Eliminating Educational Segregation in the Nation's Capital—1951–1955." *The Annals of the American Academy of Political and Social Science, Racial Desegregation and Integration*, 304 (March 1956): 98–108. https://www.jstor.org/stable/1032111.

Parker, Franklin. "Education in the Federation of Rhodesia and Nyssaland." *The Journal of Negro Education*, 30, no. 3 (Summer 1961): 286–93. https://www.jstor.org/stable/2294317.

Parrish, C. H. "Desegregation in Public Education—A Critical Summary." *The Journal of Negro Education*, 24, no. 3 (Summer 1955): 382–87. http://www.jstor.org/stable/2293467.

Patterson, Frederick D. "Duplication of Facilities and Resources of Negro Church-Related Colleges." *The Journal of Negro Education*, 29, no. 3 (Summer 1960): 368–76. https://www.jstor.org/stable/2293655.

Pearson, Richard. "Samuel Lubell, Public Opinion Analyst, Dies." *Washington Post*, August 23, 1987. https://www.washingtonpost.com/archive/local/1987/08/23/samuel-lubell-public-opinion-analyst-dies/62f30632-5a61-429d-a44f-9b9e73daf264/?utm_term=.10a8eebb3164.

Peters, Gerhard, and John T. Woolley. "The American Presidency Project." http://www.presidency.ucsb.edu/showelection.php?year=1956.

Pritchett, Wendell E. "A National Issue: Segregation in the District of Columbia and the Civil Rights Movement at Mid-Century." (2005). Faculty Scholarship Paper 1226: 1321–33. http://scholarship.law.upenn.edu/faculty_scholarship/1226.

Reddick, L. D. "Critical Review: The Politics of Desegregation." *The Journal of Negro Education*, 31, no. 3 (Summer 1962): 414–20. https://www.jstor.org/stable/2293880.

"Resolution of the Faculty and Staff of the South Carolina State College." *The Journal of Negro Education*, 25, no. 2 (Spring 1956): 197–99. https://www.jstor.org/stable/2293591.

Robison, Sophia M. "How Effective are Current Juvenile Delinquency Programs." *The Journal of Negro Education*, 28, no. 3 (Summer 1959): 351–65. https://www.jstor.org/stable/2293114.

Smothers, Ronald. "Samuel Lubell is Dead at 76; Predicted Election Outcomes." *New York Times*, August 21, 1987. http://www.nytimes.com/1987/08/21/obituaries/samuel-lubell-is-dead-at-76-predicted-election-outcomes.html.

"Sociologist E. Franklin Frazier: 1947." *Washington Area Spark*. Accessed October 17, 2017. https://www.flickr.com/photos/washington_area_spark/8662953731.

Strong, Donald S. "The Future of the Negro Voter in the South." *The Journal of Negro Education*, 26, no. 3 (Summer 1957): 400–7. https://www.jstor.org/stable/2293423.

Smyke, Raymond J. "Problems of Teacher Supply and Demand in Africa South of the Sahara." *The Journal of Negro Education*, 30, no. 3 (Summer 1961): 334–42. http://www.jstor.org/stable/2294322.

The State Board of Control, Florida. "The Problem of Entrance Requirements for the State Universities in Florida." *The Journal of Negro Education*, 25, no. 2 (Spring 1956): 200–1. https://www.jstor.org/stable/2293592.

Thompson, Charles H. "Editorial Comment: Why a *Journal of Negro Education*?" *The Journal of Negro Education*, 1, no. 1 (April 1932): 1–4. https://www.jstor.org/stable/2292009.

———. "Editorial Comment: The Association for the Study of Negro Life and History." *The Journal of Negro Education*, 4, no. 4 (October 1935): 465–67. https://www.jstor.org/stable/2291847.
———. "The Educational and Administrative Reorganization of Hampton Institute." *The Journal of Negro Education*, 9, no. 2 (April 1940): 139–43. http://www.jstor.org/stable/2292711.
———. "Truth from the Point of View of the Editor of a Scientific Magazine." *The Journal of Negro History*, 25, no. 4 (October 1940): 450–57. http://www.jstor.org/stable/2715133.
———. "Editorial Note: The American Negro in World War I and World War II." *The Journal of Negro Education*, 12, no. 3 (July 1943): 263–67. http://www.jstor.org/stable/2293044.
———. "Editorial Comment: Race Relations in the United States: The Need for Effective Leadership." *The Journal of Negro Education*, 13, no. 1 (Winter 1944): 1–6. http://www.jstor.org/stable/2292915.
———. "Editorial Comment: How Imminent is the Outlawing of Segregation." *The Journal of Negro Education*, 20, no. 4 (Autumn 1951): 498. http://www.jstor.org/stable/2966286.
———. "Editorial Note: The Supreme Court Examines 'Separate but Equal' Schools." *The Journal of Negro Education*, 22, no. 1 (Winter 1953): 1–3. http://www.jstor.org/stable/2293618.
———. "Editorial Comment: The Negro Teacher and Desegregation of the Public Schools." *The Journal of Negro Education*, 22, no. 2 (Spring 1953): 95–101. https://www.jstor.org/stable/2293077.
———. "Editorial Comment: The Impending Court Decision." *The Journal of Negro Education*, 23, no. 1 (Winter 1954): 1–2. http://www.jstor.org/stable/2293240.
———. "Editorial Comment: After the Supreme Court Decision—What?" *The Journal of Negro Education*, 23, no. 2 (Spring 1954): 107–8. http://www.jstor.org/stable/2293661.
———. "Editorial Comment: Next Steps in Racial Desegregation in Education." *The Journal of Negro Education*, 23, no. 3 (Summer 1954): 201–2. http://www.jstor.org/stable/2293216.
———. "Editorial Comment: Between Court Decision and Decree." *The Journal of Negro Education*, 23, no. 4 (Autumn 1954): 401–5. http://www.jstor.org/stable/2293830.
———. "Editorial Comment: Recent Briefs Submitted in the Segregation Cases." *The Journal of Negro Education*, 24, no. 1 (Winter 1955): 1–5. http://www.jstor.org/stable/2293173.
———. "Editorial Comment: Some Significant Byproducts of the May 17th Decision." *The Journal of Negro Education*, 24, no. 2 (Spring 1955): 91–92. http://www.jstor.org/stable/2293471.
———. "Editorial Comment: The Desegregation Decision—One Year Afterward." *The Journal of Negro Education*, 24, no. 3 (Summer 1955): 161–64. http://www.jstor.org/stable/2293448.
———. "Editorial Comment: The Twenty-Fifth Volume of the *Journal of Negro Education*." *The Journal of Negro Education*, 25, no. 1 (Winter 1956): 1–3. https://www.jstor.org/stable/2293119.
———. "Editorial Comment: Some Lessons of History and Common Sense." *The Journal of Negro Education*, 25, no. 2 (Spring 1956): 91–94. https://www.jstor.org/stable/2293566.
———. "Review of: *How Far the Promised Land by Walter White*." *The Journal of Negro Education*, 25, no. 2 (Spring 1956): 141–43. http://www.jstor.org/stable/2293574.
———. "Editorial Note: Educational Desegregation—1956." *The Journal of Negro Education*, 25, no. 3 (Summer 1956): 203. http://www.jstor.org/stable/2293428.
———. "Editorial Comment: The Dilemma of Negro Voters." *The Journal of Negro Education*, 25, no. 4 (Autumn 1956): 369–70. https://www.jstor.org/stable/2293264.

———. "Editorial Comment: Desegregation 1956; Prospects 1957." *The Journal of Negro Education*, 26, no. 1 (Winter 1957): 1–3. https://www.jstor.org/stable/2293315.
———. "Editorial Comment: The Gold Coast Revolution." *The Journal of Negro Education* 26, no. 2 (Spring 1957): 97–98. https://www.jstor.org/stable/2293335.
———. "Editorial Comment: The Negro Voter in the South." *The Journal of Negro Education*, 26, no. 3 (Summer 1957): 213–18. https://www.jstor.org/stable/2293403.
———. "Editorial Comment: The Civil Rights Bill of 1957." *The Journal of Negro Education*, 26, no. 4 (Autumn 1957): 433–34. https://www.jstor.org/stable/2293490.
———. "Editorial Comment: The Southern Association and Negro College Membership." *The Journal of Negro Education*, 27, no. 1 (Winter 1958): 1–3. https://www.jstor.org/stable/2293685.
———. "Editorial Comment: The 125th Anniversary of the American Baptist Home Mission Society." *The Journal of Negro Education*, 27, no. 2 (Spring 1958): 101–2. https://www.jstor.org/stable/2293727.
———. "The Negro College: In Retrospect and in Prospect." *The Journal of Negro Education*, 27, no. 2 (Spring 1958): 127–31. https://www.jstor.org/stable/2293732.
———. "Editorial Comment: With All Deliberate Speed." *The Journal of Negro Education*, 27, no. 4 (Autumn 1958): 437–38. https://www.jstor.org/stable/2293781.
———. "Editorial Comment: The Moral Issue in Desegregation." *The Journal of Negro Education*, 28, no. 1 (Winter 1959): 1–2. https://www.jstor.org/stable/2293385.
———. "Editorial Comment: Mr. Huntley's Astounding Proposal." *The Journal of Negro Education*, 28, no. 2 (Spring 1959): 85–91. https://www.jstor.org/stable/2293708.
———. "Editorial Comment: Juvenile Delinquency among Negroes in the United States." *The Journal of Negro Education*, 28, no. 3 (Summer 1959): 187–90. https://www.jstor.org/stable/2293099.
———. "Editorial Comment: Civil Rights in the United States." *The Journal of Negro Education*, 28, no. 4 (Autumn 1959): 389–93. https://www.jstor.org/stable/2293595.
———. "Editorial Comment: Some Unfinished Business for the 1960s." *The Journal of Negro Education*, 29, no. 1 (Winter 1960): 1–6. https://www.jstor.org/stable/2293540.
———. "Editorial Comment: Desegregation Pushed off Dead Center." *The Journal of Negro Education*, 29, no. 2 (Spring 1960): 107–11. https://www.jstor.org/stable/2293146.
———. "Editorial Note: The Negro Private and Church-Related College." *The Journal of Negro Education*, 29, no. 3 (Summer 1960): 211–16. http://www.jstor.org/stable/2293636.
———. "The Present Status of the Negro Private and Church-Related College." *The Journal of Negro Education*, 29, no. 3 (Summer 1960): 227–44. https://www.jstor.org/stable/2293638.
———. "Editorial Comment: Howard University Changes Leadership." *The Journal of Negro Education*, 29, no. 4 (Autumn 1960): 409–11. https://www.jstor.org/stable/2294210.
———. "Editorial Comment: African Education South of the Sahara." *The Journal of Negro Education*, 30, no. 3 (Summer 1961): 173–79. https://www.jstor.org/stable/2294305.
———. "Editorial Comment: The Need for More 'Deliberate Speed' in School Desegregation." *The Journal of Negro Education*, 30, no. 4 (Autumn 1961): 365–67. https://www.jstor.org/stable/2294048.
———. "Editorial Comment: The Relative Significance of the Negro Population in the United States." *The Journal of Negro Education*, 31, no. 1 (Winter 1962): 1–3. https://www.jstor.org/stable/2294530.
———. "Editorial Comment: The Southern Association and the Predominately Negro High School and College." *The Journal of Negro Education*, 31, no. 2 (Spring 1962): 105–7. https://www.jstor.org/stable/2294018.
———. "Editorial Note: The Negro Public College." *The Journal of Negro Education*, 31, no. 3 (Summer 1962): 215–20. https://www.jstor.org/stable/2293859.

———. "Editorial Comment: A Valedictory Note." *The Journal of Negro Education*, 32, no. 3 (Summer 1963): 205–7. https://www.jstor.org/stable/2294363.

Trent, Jr., W. J., and F. D. Patterson. "Financial Support of the Private Negro College." *The Journal of Negro Education*, 27, no. 3 (Summer 1958): 398–405. https://www.jstor.org/stable/2293774.

US Commission on Civil Rights. *Report of the United States Commission on Civil Rights*. Washington, DC: US Government Printing Office, 1959.

Valien, Preston. "The Desegregation Decision—One Year Afterward—A Critical Summary." *The Journal of Negro Education*, 24, no. 3 (Summer 1955): 388–96. http://www.jstor.org/stable/2293468.

———. "The Status of Educational Desegregation, 1956: A Critical Summary." *The Journal of Negro Education*, 25, no. 3 (Summer 1956): 359–68. http://www.jstor.org/stable/2293446.

Virginia Foundation for the Humanities. "Holly Knoll." http://www.aahistoricsitesva.org/items/show/208.

Watson, Denise. "If the Civil Rights Movement had a home, it was here." *The Virginian-Pilot*, February 20, 2011. https://pilotonline.com/guides/african-american-today/article_2f6a81f0-584c-54dc-b99e-5da0cda9dfa0.html.

Weaver, Robert C. "The Negro Private and Church-Related College: A Critical Summary." *The Journal of Negro Education*, 29, no. 3 (Summer 1960): 394–400. https://www.jstor.org/stable/2293658.

Wheeler, John H. "Apartheid Implemented by Education in South Africa." *The Journal of Negro Education*, 30, no. 3 (Summer 1961): 241–50. https://www.jstor.org/stable/2294312.

Wilkins, Roy. "The Future of the Negro Voter in the United States." *The Journal of Negro Education*, 26, no. 3 (Summer 1957): 424–31. https://www.jstor.org/stable/2293426.

Wilson, Frank T. "The Future of Missionary Enterprise in Africa South of the Sahara." *The Journal of Negro Education*, 30, no. 3 (Summer 1961): 324–33. https://www.jstor.org/stable/2294321.

Wright, Stephen J. "The Future of the Negro Private College: Philosophy and Program." *The Journal of Negro Education*, 27, no. 3 (Summer 1958): 406–13. https://www.jstor.org/stable/2293775.

Index

About the Author

Louis Ray is an associate professor at Fairleigh Dickinson University's Peter Sammartino School of Education and the author of *Charles H. Thompson: Policy Entrepreneur of the Civil Rights Movement, 1932–1954*, winner of the American Educational Studies Association's Critics' Choice Book Award (2013).